10,001

Mission 10,001 — Earth

a handbook for survival...
of man

Ralph Dickson Yaney, M.D., Psychoanalyst

SURYA PRESS
Malibu, California

Dedicated to:

Souls unborn who have tried to be born
Souls waiting patiently to be born
Souls borne on by wings

With love from
the chelas who
dared to care.

Heartfelt thanks to all who have made it possible to publish this book... especially to my wife and twin flame Lucile for her close direction; and to Ann Ebert as editor; to Kaye Ann Loy for research and assistance, and a special gratitude to Meredith Nugent and to Harold Steinman for in-depth research; and to the entire Summit University Press for their release of the Dictations; and to many others of all levels known and unknown.

Surya Press

Editor: Ann M. Ebert

Research
    Meredith Nugent
    Harold Steinman
    Kaye Ann Loy

Illustrations
    Ilana Myers-Pollyea

Typography
    Kalligraphics, Canoga Park, California
Printing
    Parker and Sons, Los Angeles, California
Cover
    Photo-Arts, Woodland Hills, California

Table of Contents

Part I

A Story

Seated in the antechamber, Soul R14X awaits the Karmic Board's review to offer him his new mission. The antechamber, richly appointed, inspiring inner quiet, is softly bathed in an electric-blue radiance, source unseen — different from the familiar violet-fire glowing in the etheric crystal chambers of his home, Venus.

Sensing a mild anxiety coursing through his solar plexus, he knows he should not have been called so soon. There were 2,000,602 souls ahead of him on that list, although he is aware his former record placed him near the head of his own soul group in attainment. His light body radiating this fact and authority was even acknowledged by the antechamber guard who did not challenge his entrance. Still, why now?

He had been called away from an important energy implanting project on a Venusian moon with too few available souls to comfortably continue the project and now... his thoughts trail off.

R, with a personal mild reprimand, pulls himself back into his heart meditation to prepare for the light intensity of his meeting with the Board, and he falls mentally silent.

The electric-blue light of the room now blends with a tinge of etheric rose that seems to emanate from his heart center, and a faint trace of rose perfume drifts throughout the room. He settles for a time within.

The mist atmosphere of the chamber shimmers briefly to the liquid tone of a tiny crystal bell of a single note. It reminds him of an earthly Buddhist monastery he once visited. Abruptly a tall, feminine, angelic being forms out of the blue mist. "Soul R14X, the Council is ready to receive you."

He rises. In this precise moment of no-time-oneness, he turns to an earthly vibration that has caught his etheric third eye, and reviews the records of a young earthly couple.

Monique, 23, secretary to a doctor, tugs at the sleeve of Joe sleepily, "I could stay here forever, it's so beautiful." The smell of pines is everywhere. The air is crisp, a cool 45°, the heater toasty warm. Joe's '64 vintage Porsche purrs back its contentment as they climb together up a winding mountain road in the High Sierras.

Joe, a third year Loyola law student, wonders out loud why they are always rushing to get somewhere. For once there is a little time. A three-day weekend and here they are, racing up an unknown mountain road to nowheresville, just to camp out. He falls silent and muses to himself. She feels real good, quite a gal, Monique. Something deep about her. I don't feel the rough edges; in fact, maybe better be careful. I've never experienced this before. An everyday girl more than two weeks running is usually boring, but not this one. And this, now after six months.

"Joe, look at what I brought for you." Digging into her purse, Monique extracts a baby rattle found on her last antique jaunt.

"Wow," Joe, perplexed. "Never know what you're going to do next! What am I supposed to do with that?"

"Oh, Joe, it's simple. Have baby, will rattle!"

"Wait a minute! You have to get married first."

"Oh, Joe, I wondered if you'd ever ask!"

Corny, but feels good.

Scanning deeper, R14X flashes through a brief life profile.

Monique, 23, born January 29, 1955: emotionally stable, non-neurotic, mild hysterical personality — insignificant maladaptive behavior, emotional body intact; no drug history of significance, brief experiment with smoking; open, friendly, loves life, people and animals; father — solid, spiritual background; mother — warm, slightly neurotic, good mothering; religious background — ambivalent Protestant faith, some childhood teachings; mental body very alert, four-plus, capable of great growth, can be stimulated; etheric body — no damage to the soul sheath, minor problem from her present lifetime experience through jazz music of her culture; fortunately, no rock music damage.

Past life records: ancient Lemurian priestess sacrificed by the Dark Forces when refused to leave her post; 1653, a nun in France, very devoted and much attainment; 1850, mother of a large family, Catholic religion. Certain negative records have been transmuted.

Joe, 28 years, born May 8, 1951: Loyola law student, bright, slightly compulsive tendency toward concrete thinking; some curiosity about Eastern religions, childhood Catholic training and brief episode of experimentation with yoga; etheric body intact; emotional body well developed but slightly blocked, mild obsessive-compulsive neurosis; childhood trauma from over-strict fathering; good mothering; mental body excellent, slight damage from smoking during college and military service; physical body strong, minor damage from sugar intake during childhood, addicted to ice cream; etheric intact, no drug experience except one episode with marijuana which caused tear in solar plexus chakra, now healed from the perfected tone of Hail Mary mantras given in devotion by his genetic mother.

Past life records: excellent attainment, monk in Eastern Buddhist monastery — high initiations; served with King Arthur's court as a knight; served with Columbus as crew. Father of large family, early 1900's, Columbus, Ohio, Catholic; negative records ready for transmutation except strong pride and intellectual

*attitudes; karmically attached to Renaissance lifetime
of law practice at University of Cologne.*

"Joe, I love you, but you know, joking aside, I have the
strangest feeling right now. I am excited about us, but it is
almost as if something very important is trying to happen
and we are a part of it. I don't know where I am getting
these feelings! What's happening?"

"Monique, you know, I think you're right. I've got a
very warm feeling right now and I don't know what it
means. Almost as if sitting on top of this mountain
someone upstairs is personally, directly involved with us.
And I know enough about psychology to be wary of my
own omnipotent wish to be important — but why us? I'm
not that important; maybe we are. Anyhow, I wish
someone could tune in and let us in on what's going on."

Monique, snuggling up. "It's a good feeling, even if
everyone up there knows about us."

At home in Monique's apartment three weeks later fixing
spaghetti dinner, Monique, still high from the mountain
camping trip, fondly teases Joe. "I could have stayed on
the mountain forever. In fact, I was so high I don't even
mind our calculated gamble; and you know, it's strange,
but I don't even care if I am pregnant."

Long pause. "I sure hope not. I've got to get started
in my new law firm before I can think of kids."

"Don't worry. Dr. Johnson said he'd put an IUD in me
next week so there won't be any more Russian roulette. I
don't really like that thing, but I guess it's the safest
answer."

"I don't think the doctors really know what makes
that thing work, but it is a foreign body irritant and fools
the uterus into thinking it must reject whatever is in it; so
even if a fertilized egg implants, it will abort spontane-
ously. So I guess it's okay — although some women
continually bleed."

"Joe, for heaven's sake! What a depressing thought. I'm not sure now if I want that thing."

In the etheric chamber, a gavel raps a ringing note on a crystal table. An authoritative being steps forward to address the council. His robe — violet, sealed in front with a purple apron, softly emblazoned with diamonds — flashes living-laser rays throughout the room and...the universe. Voices in the chamber resound together in hushed tones like that of a great earthly organ in triple pianissimo, then fall quickly silent.

"Brothers and Sisters of the Karmic Board: We have before us a most urgent plea, a call for assistance from the few enlightened souls on Terra to send in the balance of the 10,001 Avatars without delay. The cosmic cycle of 2000 is rapidly approaching, the balance of light and darkness is holding, but barely, and unless some of the 10,001 get into incarnation soon, the cycle may be lost and with it the evolutionary platform of Terra in its present state. The Dark Forces are stepping up their war against the light and are meeting our thrusts with greater darkness.

"Free souls everywhere on earth are falling prey to the consciousness and philosophy engineered by Lucifer and his rebellious, fallen band. There are almost no souls on Terra free from this infiltration deep within their consciousness. The strong foothold of socialism and communism has succeeded in destroying older souls trained to bring in God-government. Now over one-half of the planet is in darkness, and more nations are under attack on the inner and outer and in threat of succumbing each passing day.

"There is grave danger to the planet as an evolutionary platform if souls of light cannot be awakened by the teaching of the Avatars. And this does not even take note of the great karma to earthbound soul evolutions if they continue to encumber themselves with the murder of souls of light, ignoring of the prophets, the messengers, and even Mother Mary herself, particularly her Fatima prophecy and her abundant miracles.

"These souls are rapidly losing all ability to discern, to separate truth from error, even light from darkness."

Briefly, his aura flames a soft purple-gold, and he continues.

"We have in the antechamber awaiting audience one whom we have called to volunteer for Terra — R14X, whom you all know. He is one of our most able adepts, presently serving in his native planet, Venus. His record of service is well known to all of you. He is particularly important to us at this time because of his advanced knowledge of cosmic law and his ability to translate it into human consciousness gained from his former lifewave on Terra. His success in serving under Columbus as boatswain aboard the Santa Maria — rendering invaluable assistance to hierarchy in quieting the Dark Forces working through the threatened mutiny of the crew, which would have aborted Saint Germain's important mission as Columbus — makes him most qualified for this mission. His subsequent imprisonment and death attempting to defend his master, Saint Germain, was exemplary.

"Unfortunately, only 22% out of the 2,500 Avatars we have sent in have been able to remain in embodiment. The advanced scientific methods of birth control on Terra, particularly the birth control pills, have prevented conception in those parents most eligible for parenting the Avatars, and the high degree acceptance of this method among the so-called sophisticates have really held out the 10,001.

"We are behind schedule. Our alternative choices are less hopeful of bearing fruit. We could utilize less sensitive parent souls and those with less attainment; or we could give up on our special dispensation of these souls to American parents and try other nations. And all of you know the odds of this, with the godless society of socialism and communism spreading over the planet. We can't risk the programming of the Avatars in those countries dominated by communism and the subsequent damage to auras of light by implantation of fear and terrorism — so much the main tactic of the Dark Force and boldly expressed by their instruments Marx, Lenin, and Stalin and successors. We will, however, not explore this area until we learn there is no hope of getting these souls into American parents where the etheric blueprint of freedom has been set.

"Before our Council today is even a heavier problem, and that is how to counterbalance the Herod Plot that has gained public acceptance in America and, sadly, legal credibility in the United States Supreme Court.

"This is part of our consideration in sending in R14X at this time. The problem is not simple, since the massacre of the life of the soul in the womb occurs in a lifewave at a time when the soul least expects it, is least prepared, and is emotionally most vulnerable. The record left in the etheric memory of this type of violent death seems to have greater impact and damage than the Avatar volunteers recognize. Master Hilarion, in charge of the healing ray, has asked to speak to you briefly about this problem."

"Thank you, Chairman and Members of the Board. Since it has fallen to me to assist in the healing process of the damaged etheric and emotional bodies of these souls, I would like you to understand the time element of recuperation as related to earth time. I am finding it takes at least three earth years for a soul, even of adept status, to heal the etheric tear in the etheric membrane, particularly surrounding the emotional solar plexus chakra. This time factor is most disturbing. Even though the will and dedication of these souls is most powerful and they desire to return immediately to another incarnation for God-service, they cannot until the etheric web is

healed and the record of the pain transmuted. Otherwise, immediate return would result in a damaged
emotional body and an inability to carry out their earthly
mission, even if they made it on a second try, a second
incarnation.

"The worst records to heal are the saline abortions,
a slow death from burning of the skin with acid in the
womb, and the six-month-plus dismemberings and
decapitations. These souls suffer so long there is literally
engraved in their etheric light memory bodies this
experience, rendering return impossible until the angelic
workers have been able to repair these massive etheric
tears and the records transmuted by the souls themselves in the inner temples.

"Most of the 10,001 so aborted have handled this
experience as the initiation of the crucifixion and have
come through victorious. However, some have not done
so well, and these souls are presently in our retreats for
recuperation and healing, but may miss the return earth
cycle for incarnation."

"Thank you, Master Hilarion, for your report. The
problem directly before the Board today is the need to
risk sending in Soul R14X or to hold him back until we
have a more secure base on Terra before risking such an
advanced soul.

"If we hold him back and wait, things may continue
to deteriorate and our chances of getting him in later will
worsen — balanced against the potential risk to his soul
body if he is aborted on his mission. We also will have to
karmicly share in this damage. He almost achieved full
enlightenment and mastery during his last embodiment
on Terra and will certainly achieve it this time, unless he
loses all support during his early growth years. We have
to balance in our deliberations this potential loss against
the gain for the planet's evolution if his mission included
in '10,001' achieves what has been planned.

"The Angel of Record is ready to speak to you about the potential parents of Soul R14X's sojourn on Terra and the risk to the mission."

"Gracious Members of the Board: We have located two souls of light who have tentatively agreed to parent Soul R14X, and they are presently waiting in an adjoining anteroom for a soul meeting with him and the Maha Chohan.

"Our Recording Angels have noted that the mother, known on Terra as Monique, is well qualified from former records and is well prepared for the task of motherhood. Her experience as a Catholic nun in the French monastery has firmly set her soul's devotion toward God and kindled a deep respect for hierarchy.

"We wish to call to your attention the one defect, which is a tendency to trust someone with greater knowledge than herself implicitly because of his title without questioning and testing first through her heart center. This neurosis, as Terra psychologists would describe, came from her devout but harsh testing in the French monastery and is carried over to her present lifetime. The doctor, however, for whom she serves as secretary may tell her to have an abortion, and she might well act on it. She has had insufficient spiritual and religious training in this lifetime to assist her in making a right choice. On the positive side, she has a strong will for right action and a very well-developed and balanced emotional body with excellent intuitive responses. She has an intact etheric body and has demonstrated to our advanced angelic representatives of Archangel Gabriel that she can be reached and will respond to our contact.

"Regarding the potential father, Joseph, known on Terra as Joe Bishop, the problem is more complex. Basically he is very strong and is a natural protector, much like the tradition of his namesake, Joseph. He is rapidly evolving in his present lifestream and dharmic choice as a law student. The conflicts occur in areas of pride of profession and desire for earthly approval of his intellectual attainment. This stems from an unresolved record of a lifetime in law at the University of Cologne in which he entered into an intense dispute with a Fellow of the Bar. This same soul is now present as one of his teachers at his law school and there is a karmic replay in action. Neither has used the Law of Forgiveness. This could well tip the balance in favor of an abortion. He may view the pregnancy in his outer mind as interfering with his need to demonstrate perfection to his former rival, now his law teacher.

"Balanced against this action is a positive karma with Soul R14X, having served together on the Santa Maria with Saint Germain, which may intuitively cause him to think twice about such a dire action to abort. It is quite close, and we cannot determine the direction of his action at this time. His attainment is above average. His Catholic background might tip the balance in favor of R14X."

"Thank you, Recording Angel. Beloved members of our Board, I have presented in some detail this case before you today, but it is not just this individual case that is at stake today. Unfortunately, what you have heard is typical of the whole problem we are facing on Terra, and the threat, to put it bluntly, is the *abortion of a planet and a people.*

"We all know too well that a negative left-hand choice of Monique and Joseph to abort this soul mission of Soul R14X inadvertently will have far-reaching consequences for many souls and lifestreams. The karmic weight alone of aborting an Avatar of R14X's stature will be so heavy personally for both that it may prevent their return to Terra for some time and perhaps also delay their evolution for several lifetimes. And the karma may have to be personally paid back by their own abortion or sterility in future embodiments. If insufficient time is left in the evolutionary platform of Terra, this may well mean the abortion of their own Divine Plan — a very heavy karmic price and a loss to all of us, since both souls are advanced on the path, although they have not made contact with our hierarchy yet in this lifetime.

"We have an additional problem. Because of R14X's attainment, the karmic weight for the planet of his crucifixion en utero will have to be shared by the American people as a group. This will mean further flooding, cataclysms, and weather unbalancing, which will be used by the Dark Forces as evidence of God's lack of caring for his children, and they will lead more children of light into darkness.

"Unfortunately, we would not be able to honor the requests of responsible sons and daughters on Terra to hold back such karma. To do so would require a balancing of energy payment somewhere, and it would simply add to further gravitational weight which would tip the planet to 4.25° out of axis, which you know from Master Hilarion and Master Cuzco's dissertations would exceed the present maximum 4° limit. This cannot be allowed to occur. It would take the planet out of orbit in a wobbling vibrational spin. Then we would have the abortion of a planet and a people and the final destruction of the evolutionary platform for earth-attached souls to complete their initiation and path, to say nothing of the balance in the solar system that depends on earth's victory in the light.

"Brothers of the Board, I put before you your decision about Soul R14X's mission at this time and the alternate plan of sending in a soul or souls of lesser attainment in advance of him where the karma of an abortion would be less; but, of course, the alternate would not carry his potential for bringing the planet closer to the cosmic timetable of earth year 2000."

The chamber falls silent. The ritual of personal deliberation convenes. A sweet smoke gently spirals upward. The tender offering of many acceptable prayers from faithful sons and daughters of God embodied on Terra and from those out of embodiment in the etheric retreats fill the room as urgent requests for mercy and for the Board to send reinforcements from the 10,001. This tips the balance as one by one the aura of each Council member brightens into a special golden hue — automatically signaling an affirmative vote. Kuan Yin, a grand feminine being of authority, rises with her personal vote of support for the mission. The room burns with a golden light — a unanimous vote.

The gavel descends. The Karmic Board stamps the application of R14X's mission to Terra, *MISSION AUTHORIZED*. It needs now only his approval and the approval of both his parents-to-be plus the Maha Chohan to proceed with the mission.

CHAIRMAN: "A point of information is in order in this case. Some of our advisors have questioned the use of an unmarried couple for this mission. Unfortunately, most of the married couples of sufficient attainment are limiting their families because they have absorbed the brainwashing of the Dark Forces' infiltration and believe they are helping mankind, since they have been told the lie that by the year 2000 there will not be enough food to feed the population of the planet. It's painfully clear that they know nothing of God's cycles, the laws of abundance and of souls recycling off the planet as evolved evolutions in light bodies. It's apparent they do not even know of other levels of existence beyond time and space.

"Some of our Avatars have been waiting in the auras of their assigned parents for as long as four years, and in the older mothers, they may not get in before the hormonal cycles of life below close the door.

"I feel it necessary for the record to state that had a married couple of sufficient attainment been discovered with appropriate karmic ties and properly balanced four lower bodies, we would have certainly used them. Some of the married couples considered had attached themselves to rigid worldly biases that would tend to force the evolution of R14X into a similar channel which would effectively limit his mission. While they undoubtedly would protect his fetal life, they would abort the mission at a later point. No couple of sufficient attainment has been located. Several were seriously considered, but for multiple reasons they were marked unacceptable.

"Souls of this magnitude require considerable parental wisdom. Because of their attainment and mental and emotional sensitivity, they are most difficult children to raise. In a rigid home environment, insensitive parents may well destroy the sensitive, creative instrument they want to protect, and a valuable embodiment would be lost. Placing such a soul into a less restrictive home without definite moral values has often the same result, and the exposure to drugs and hard music completes the abortion of a mission.

"With the legal acceptance of abortion in America and the use of abortion as a back-up contraceptive, members of the Board, we are facing a major crisis in Mission 10,001! The plot is an old one, repeated many times before, and has contributed to the fall of other Golden Age civilizations. For our convenience, it is labeled 'The Herod Plot,' as it operated in Jesus' mission. So far, in the past seven years, this tactic has kept out of embodiment twenty million souls in America alone and approximately 25% of the 10,001 before they could render service. This is a greater loss of souls of light than in the last three major wars on Terra.

"For the benefit of our chelas in training, listening to this proceeding on the etheric wave system, I want to remind you that even an Avatar in embodiment while still in the womb starts to render service to a planet and a people. Not only does he have to maintain a certain stability of consciousness to allow the fullest development of the atomic structure in his physical body, but he must also maintain his cosmic alignment to allow this young body and the atomic structure to radiate the maximum amount of light. This starts at the moment of conception within the very atoms composing his body and is intensified moment by moment.

"You will recall in the case of Master Jesus that the moment Jesus was present in Mary's womb her face shone like a sun. This fact is well understood by the Dark Force. So they have deceived mankind into accepting population control, deluding them into believing that a fetus is not a soul and that it is an act of kindness to the mother to cut the fetus out as if it were a cancer, which light indeed is to the Dark Force. They know of the prophecy that the light will swallow up the darkness.

"The Dark Forces recognize their urgent need to take these great souls of light out of embodiment immediately, because the longer these souls of great light are on Terra, the shorter the time for souls of darkness, as prophesied and measured by the simple ratio of light to darkness.

"The Dark Forces also know of the return of the karma to mankind that will come as the result of these crucifixions, and they will manipulate it as evidence of a cruel, vindictive God without love. This manipulation will pull more souls of light into their dark ways. Earth children are slow to learn that darkness hates the light.

"Incidently, for the benefit of the new chela students, soul R14X is, as you may have ascertained by now, a code name used for the purpose of preventing the Dark Force with their computers from tuning into the soul vibration in environments less protected than this. The advanced soul name contains certain substantive fohatic keys to a soul's attainment and records and would be used negatively by the Dark Force if this were made available.

"Because of the increasing complexity of survival of soul life on Terra, in 1962 our Board gave forth a special dispensation which has held back certain souls of darkness from embodiment on Terra until the Holy Christ Children could embody. These Holy Christ Children are advanced, evolved souls of light attainment and are hated and feared by the Sons of Belial and souls of darkness, who are now determined to take them out of embodiment. In 1973 another dispensation was granted to send in the 10,001 Avatars, and a few are now successfully serving in young bodies. As you know, we have called this dispensation *MISSION 10,001 EARTH.*"

K-17 of the Cosmic Secret Service reports.

"The Dark Forces working through reembodied Atlantean scientists on Terra are about ready to release a tasteless chemical that can be secretly placed in a municipal water supply causing immediate abortion of all intrauterine pregnancies of up to three weeks. This is a plot similar to the use of a special fluoride chemical introduced legally into earth water supplies and tooth paste, the same chemical Hitler perfected to break the will of concentration camp prisoners. Because such an early chemical abortion would appear simply as an irregular menstrual flow, it would go generally unnoticed and, therefore, has a high priority with the D.F. Unfortunately, the density in earth children is such that they care more for the permanency of their teeth than their brains!

"So our problems are increasing, particularly how to reeducate mankind and to warn children of the light of these problems before the cycle of opportunity is lost. They have already developed a long-lasting, injectible contraceptive that is now openly available. Thank you, Brothers and Sisters of the Board," and K-17's aura receeds from the chamber.

"Brothers of the Light, the Maha Chohan desires a hearing regarding Soul R14X."

"My Brothers and Sisters, I have just come from a meeting with R14X and the souls of his parents-to-be, Monique and Joseph Bishop. All have solemnly agreed to the mission and have given their vows. Joseph particularly warmly greeted R14X. He recognized him as one of his loyal boatswains of his former command when, as third mate, he served on the Santa Maria with Columbus. He was most honored to be offered this opportunity; and the mother, Monique, was ecstatic to be given such a high soul.

"I, as the representative of the Holy Spirit, am well pleased for the success of this mission. However, I did not give an unqualified yes vote, as required, but abstained until I could ask for a special dispensation from the Board to assist in this mission.

"If someone among mankind can be located to teach this couple ere three months lapse and provide a direct contact with hierarchy, I can then give my yea vote for this mission of R14X."

CHAIRMAN: "Send K-17's legions out immediately to locate a Son of Wisdom for this couple's evolution and initiation."

"Dr. Johnson, I feel so light today, almost walking on clouds!"

"It must be the weather, nothing good has happened around here for a month. By the way, when do you want me to put in your IUD?"

"I've been thinking I shouldn't use it. Have you got any other ideas?"

"Only the pill, and you don't seem to go for that either. Nothing left except the diaphragm, which doesn't always work; or just don't do it — that works, too.

Incidentally, when was your last period?"

"About five weeks ago."

"Not irregular, are you?"

"No, just a little late this time."

"Well, no problem, Monique. Let me slip in the IUD now and if you are pregnant, you soon won't be. It's the right time, anyway."

"Joe, you know a funny thing happened. Dr. Johnson wanted to put an IUD in me today and it really seemed like the right thing to do, since I am over one week late anyway. But as I started to undress I had the strongest feeling, just like that time driving up the mountain, like somebody was tuned into me. I could almost hear a soul talking and telling me, 'Don't do it; there is too much at stake. I've got to get through.' It was so real I had to sit down, it surprised me so. I don't even know if I am pregnant, but I think I am. My breasts seem fuller — but that sensation, knowing someone is there again."

"Monique, I'm glad you didn't use that IUD, but if you're pregnant, I'm going to have a lot to worry about. I really want to marry you, but I don't like the idea of being forced into it by a pregnancy. That's just not my way. Besides, getting married right now, having a baby on top of my coming bar exam is just too rough. I've got to turn in a good showing to Professor Klein for that law firm he knows about so he will recommend me for a good position, and you know how sticky that guy is. Anyhow, maybe you're not pregnant and we are worrying for nothing. So get Dr. Johnson to give you a test next week."

"Joe, wake up! I just had a crazy dream and I want to tell you about it."

"Oh, Monique, okay, what is it?"

"It seemed like I went to this beautiful mansion and there were all these little children, all so beautiful, playing in the flowers and grass around the mansion. A tall woman dressed in a pure white linen dress, almost radiant, came up to me and said, 'These are your children.' I said, 'How wonderful! I will love them forever.' There must have been a hundred children playing there. They were so beautiful, almost translucent, like jewels. However, it puzzled me, since I don't have any children. She said, 'Don't worry, these are your children. You have been a good mother and you must continue to be a good mother. One of these children needs you now, and more children will be yours if you take care of this one.'

"Then she took me inside and we walked up the longest spiral staircase I have ever seen to the very top of the mansion. At the top . . . it was as if the roof opened into the universe, and I saw a man, whose body and face was shining like a sun, walking toward me saying, "Mother,' and I awoke."

"Whew! I may have had some analysis in the past, but I can't analyze that one. I think you've got kids on the brain!"

"Oh, Joe, you're not taking me seriously."

"Oh, yes I am! It just scares me to think about it. The possibility of you being pregnant! And so many kids! Somewhere I remember something about the house in a dream representing your own self, your own accomplishments. I don't know what the spiral staircase is except it seems to be taking you up to some high place."

"Yes, it sure was high, and the man calling me 'Mother' looked like someone from another world. He was all light, like Michaelangelo's paintings of Jesus after his ascension. And why did he call me 'Mother'?"

"Got me, Monique. Anyhow, call me at work and let me know how the test comes out."

"Monique, I know you were told it was positive, but sometimes they make mistakes. Better get another one. I just don't see how we can start our life out with a pregnancy."

"Joe, I really love you, but I love this thing inside me too, and I don't want to lose either of you."

"I know, Monique, but be sensible. We just can't start out like this. My law career has to be most important right now. I think you'd better have an abortion. I talked to a clinic the other day, and they can do it easy as an outpatient, as long as you're under two months. They do it by suction; it's painless to the mother."

"Okay, I'll think some more about it."

"Monique, where have you been? I've been looking and calling all over for you. Dr. Johnson said you took the afternoon off. I even went to the Abortion Clinic, hoping you didn't go."

"I started to, but my feet knew better."

"After this morning, Monique, I called up my old analyst to check on your dream, and frankly I was kind of uptight. He wasn't in his office any more and the person answering the phone said he had moved back East but asked if he could help. He sounded warm on the phone, so I took a chance and went over. When I entered his office, I felt a peculiar tingling sensation like fine rain on my skin, and a sense of deep calm. The room was ordinary enough and he was very pleasant. He had the most penetrating blue eyes I had ever seen. They were kind, but it was the way he looked at me!

"Before I got too deep into what I wanted to find out, I checked out his credentials: M.D. of a top Western university and best residency training in Psychiatry and member of one of the best Psychoanalytic Institutes, so I didn't ask him too much more except if he could tell me what kind of analysis he practiced. His answers didn't help much, since he said he used all schools but leaned more towards a Jungian approach, and something about 'Soul Analysis.'

"Before we started to work, he asked me if I knew why I had come to him — strange question. Then he asked me if I knew him from some other place — strange question number two. And then he asked me if there was a new person in my life that I wanted to talk about. That did it. So I got right in and worked on our relationship and your pregnancy.

"Then I gave him your dream and, of all things, he asked me to analyze it as if it were my own dream. I kept trying to tell him it wasn't my dream, but he kept right on interpreting as if he didn't hear me.

"When we got to the part where you ascended the spiral staircase, he asked me to let myself go completely. Then he put me on the couch and asked me what did I see. This blew my mind because I saw myself on this staircase beside you and this magnificent man of light coming towards us with his arms outstretched with a beautiful smile on his face. I couldn't speak. You know, I think this man is our son, and I think we were given advance warning up in the mountain just like you said, and he is somehow a very important person.

"The analyst seemed to agree and went on to explain the spiral staircase as our initiations we are carving upward on our own path, which is an ever-ascending spiral of light energy. And the children are like the expanding, transcending, creative products of a perfect union of the soul with God, like an evolving marriage of two kindred souls here and now.

"Anyway, I'm sure glad I found you before we did something we would forever regret. This guy I want you to meet. He sure isn't like my first analyst. Seems like I've known him for a long time. I've never heard of a psychoanalyst performing a marriage but who knows, maybe!

"The thing I can't get over is the electric energy in that room. It did something to me. It seemed that the energy was the same feeling that we had on the mountain."

Part II

*The author invites you to be his guest
on an inner journey, and to consider
the story you have just read as fact...*

and to now consider Part II of this
light voyage
as perhaps
knowledge
waiting
for
the
Word
in
your
heart

1.
The Great Silent Invisible War

INVISIBLE

The Prophecy of a War to Come

Through a dulled consciousness somewhere within his psyche, but dimly registered, man knows he has been told by the prophets that there is a war going on — a war of Armageddon — and there is to be a judgment of something in process.

And, intellectually, an explanation of the war of Armageddon springs forth, but it will not be of much help.

For the record anyway:

The war of Armageddon is a war between good and evil.

a war between forces of light and darkness,

a war on the inner and outer consciousness,

a war between cycles of life and cycles of death consciousness,

a war between forces committed to evolution of the soul and forces committed to destruction of the soul,

a battle for souls of light at all levels,

a war now in progress,

a war fought by Archangels of Light and the legions of the Lord with the assistance of the evolving souls, their astral fallen angels, and the Satanic forces fighting for unevolved souls of light and the energy, the free light, their souls contain.

But with eyes scaled and dimmed, man fumbles and asks, "Where is the war?" He muses it will be in some distant time when he is no longer here, or maybe it is just a myth. It is too much for him to understand, and too complicated.

"But wait," speaks a small voice from deep within.

Slaughter by the Number

Somehow man has been conditioned to only counting numbers lost in a war, not human lives with personalities, and no longer looks at the endless rows of crosses in a military cemetary, preferring burial without markers. He still considers, with a shudder, the Civil War loss of nearly one million souls and World Wars I and II with nearly one and one-half more million American sons sacrificed.[1] These are numbers only. The human mind rebels and recoils at a request to recall this terror, these violent deaths, and just simply refuses. He desires to go on living and to forget, hoping this cannot occur again. War is so horrible its meaning cannot be encompassed within the psyche of struggling, evolving man. Until finally accepting as reality mechanized-computerized thinking, he looks at the potential of nuclear war by reducing life to mock numbers — 1+ mil, 2+ mil deaths estimated.

Numbly, man with unseeing, opened eyes looks at the statistics of 120 mil, 120,000,000 souls murdered by the Communists[2] in their country-by-country takeover since 1917 — USSR, Estonia, Lativa, Poland, Hungary, Czechoslovakia, China, Tibet, Cuba, North and South Vietnam, Cambodia, and sixty-seven others![3] And he barely notes the threat of loss of 17 million more Taiwan souls to be turned over to a Communist purge as his nation allies with Red China; or the systematic murder of 2.5 million Cambodians — 33% of their population[4] —

now hardly a reportable figure; and the murder of (6 mil) Jews is just obscure history.

Armageddon, the battle of the end that the prophets foretold, is somehow always seen in the future and will never happen here! Meanwhile the silent, deadly battle relentlessly grinds on, and America and the free world sleep, smug with their hoard of creature comforts, their conscience lulled by the hypnotic hum of their new, computerized, robotized superiority that makes easy the manipulation of hard facts into ciphers that were once known as souls and human persons.

And with man's concern for comfort greater than his concern for protection, he has allowed even the cradle to become endangered. America, the very cradle of civilization, is in trouble within and without.

Now, with blind, staring eyes he casually notes his own U.S. Supreme Court's decision to replace God and the Constitution by declaring the fetus in a mother's womb is not a soul or a person and can be extinguished at will.[5]

'Reverence for life' has become a whisper hardly heard. Consciously it just does not register that his own Supreme Court's decision has by tacit agreement added to the yearly world total of 55 million souls lost in abortion[6] to this incredible slaughter, the death toll of this silent, invisible war, Armageddon.

On the outer reality of consciousness, it does not even pass as a thought that he is actually now at war — a war to the bitter end with real blood, the stench of death, terror and broken nations. Strangely it does not register that openly published and openly declared the goal of Communism is to "bury free man;"[7] that the goal set forth in the Communist Manifesto is to not rest until the entire world is under the hammer of world communism and that any end, any evil, will justify the means of obtaining this goal.[8]

Free man does not understand that agreements made with this enemy will only serve the purpose of binding free man and are as pacts made with Satan himself. Detente and SALT agreements have only been clever manipulations to delude and confuse free man made with an avowed godless enemy that is an enemy of honor, of the Word, and of any form of freedom.[9] These manipulations were designed to give the enemy time to prepare for war, spending 100% more dollars than the USA, representing one-fifth of his gross national product spent on arms,[10] amazingly assisted by "loans" of 49 billion dollars from American banks.[11] And now with disdain, this invisible enemy places missiles even in Cuba without fear of reprisal from a U.S. President.[12]

And it does not stir free men into action when the record of these agreements and treaties shows 24 out of 25 broken by Russia[13] as he watches his nation continue to negotiate away future strength casually with new agreements in great fanfare and earnestness.

Or that his National Security Advisor in the Cabinet of his President has declared a need to rewrite the Constitution[14] and that "Marxism . . . is a victory of reason over belief."[15] The same Marx and disciples who have ruthlessly declared war on God, freedom, and religion and whose philosophy has determined to stamp out, with mass murder and torture, souls of light.[16] So arrogantly they somehow remain mysteriously invisible.

But free man, embarrassed, confused, feeling small and childlike, told it is wrong to think such thoughts about other forms of government and reminded that he must be fair, mumbles, fumbles and reaches for a pacifier — a beer, a martini, a cigarette or a hit, or the TV or radio with its sense-deadening rock music, or he pursues some sexual pleasure or perversion to forget the growing pain in his heart.

And he only blinks when told by a brave, disgusted, voluntarily resigned general, chief of his own Air Force Intelligence, that all the grain he sold to the USSR at a giveaway price — grain his own brothers could not buy, grain paid for by dollars from American New York banks[17] — now rests 1,000 feet deep inside hardened USSR concrete defense bunkers waiting to feed USSR troops and civilians in case of nuclear war with USA.[18] These bunkers are literally underground cities constructed at a cost of $500,000,000 each, and there are 1,500 of them in the Soviet Union![19] They are bunkers that at the negotiating table in Salt I the USSR and USA promised not to build, since they agreed nuclear war was so terrible no one would use it, so why try to defend against it.

And free man just looks dumb when he is told that when Communist Russia fire their first salvo of nuclear rockets, this first strike will incinerate and murder 160,000,000 Americans.[20] Eighty-five percent of America's population will be undefended because of his government's niave respect for the signed agreements of an omnipotent enemy — an enemy that has declared war on the planet and feels only contempt for the defenders of freedom. America historically never strikes the first blow. In America's honorable return defense strike, she is told she will only be able to destroy 5,000,000 Russians,[21] representing 2% of their population, since they have become so defensively hardened that nothing less than a direct hit on top of one of their bunkers will touch them.

Because free man has been so worried about looking good instead of watchful of the self-declared enemies of freedom and God, he has further defused his second line of defense rockets. Since it takes three days to rearm, they will be useless for a return strike.[22]

Somehow man has not been told the facts of the

war. "What war," he says. "Where is the war?" It's been here
all the time — Armageddon — but amazingly it is well
hidden, almost as if free man has been programmed not
to see it or hear it. And almost as planned, confused free
man, with fuses blown and his dulled consciousness
overloaded, is led like sheep back to a further deprog-
ramming. So back to the bottle, the pot, the coke, the jazz
and rock music, the TV, and all the perversions of sex,
since nothing is sacred anymore and nothing makes
sense anyway.

Meanwhile, this great, silent battle of Armageddon
may end without the shriek and whine of rockets flying or
the deafening roar and rumble of a nuclear mushroom,
and this too is part of the dark plan.

The Dark Force prefers to work in darkness and in
silence and to do their work quietly behind closed doors
as the American dollar shrinks with inflation and gold is
drained from the nation... and we see another quiet,
deadly silent front in this War of Armageddon.[23] The
economic blood of America is drained by a systematic
feeding and stimulation of America's greedy material
appetite.

Then, for want of a fast gallon, American man is
lulled by his oil companies into accepting lies of shortage
to artificially boost the price. As long as he gets his own
gallon, he seems unconcerned that these American
companies openly declare their disinterest in America,
and with pride say they are "international corporations"
and not responsible to America alone, then unabashedly
turn and chide American man for his greed of their own
product.

And American man — innocent, confused —
continues with undisciplined appetite, selling his soul,
his blood, his very own land to the Arabs, to the
Japanese, the Germans, the French, and even the
Communists[24] to support his rising greed and inflation.
Unemployment rises, welfare state-supported depen-

dents rise, he becomes more decadent and bureaucratically dependent, and his house collapses as nations before him have internally collapsed to a collective socialism, Communism. And he does not know what happened!

Only then will the Battle of Armageddon become loud and known when free man witnesses personally the crucifixion of his brothers of light in the Communist slave labor camps. Then, systematically, their blood and light will be extracted, and souls will be exterminated after all energy has been painfully drained for the communist state, now a godless dark planet once known as earth. All that appears left is for God to once again purify the godless civilizations beneath the waters, leaving mankind to start again from a karmic, primitive beginning on the painful upward journey of a lagging evolution, although this God has promised to man he would not repeat — not repeat in the same way.

In God's name how has this happened! This silent war, this Battle of Armageddon that Revelation foretells? Has no one heard the warnings? And why cannot America, the land of such advanced technology where the most elaborate aircraft warning systems have been developed, see or hear the sound of her own walls coming down?

At 4:00 a.m., the hour of witchcraft,[25] no word comes from the Watchman on the Wall in reply to our question. Only a thick, heavy vibration is perceived; and deep within the sleeping city is the faint grinding noise of a discotheque at work, much like the amplified sound of termites devouring the very foundation.

The Strategy and Return of the Old Herod Plot

So comes again to free man, sitting sophisticated, smug and well-pleased with his outer gain of things, the Herods of old — kings of modern times. Hearing the warning of their end as foretold by the prophets, they conspire to murder the newborn Avatars and the children of light before they can reach their maturity and complete the prophecy.

So subtly and not so subtly is the drug pusher, publicly supported, who comes to destroy the auric protection in these unsuspecting souls of light as they are promised a short-cut to higher consciousness. Also coming with them, hand-in-hand, are the jazz and rock musicians with their jagged rhythms and sense-deadening beat and strobe lights, all of which tear the aura and drive wedges into the soul forcefield, thereby guaranteeing access through hypnotic programming of the consciousness, to the drugs under which influence the music is composed and experienced. This same music, scientists have proven, will kill and destroy plant life and interfere with the natural rhythm of the human heart.[26]

Come, also, the Herod liquor vendors to anesthetize the emotional bodies and to harden and weaken the feelings, particularly the heart, and to render the soul of light unable to sense his external world or to be aware of danger from within or without.

Reigning also over forty-six million of our people are the tobacco kings[27] who control the mental body and destroy the subtle vibrations, links of memory of former lives. These Herod kings are ready on an instant to convert their cigarettes to marijuana. With their pollution of the air and the minds of the youth, they care not about the cancerous destruction of the physical body, bringing an early exit before the soul has completed his plan, or the transmitting of genetic defects to the next genera-tion.

And also to come are the purveyors of sugar and additives with the mass infusion of sugar into the diet, from baby formulas to junk food, arresting the body's ability to manufacture its own sugar, weakening the physical body, creating sugar addiction, lethargy, loss of energy, and preparing the body chemistry for later addictions of alcohol and smoking which stimulate the body chemistry similarly to sugar.[28]

And, finally, even respected legislators and doctors come to destroy a nation's offspring, believing they are assisting the evolution of man by reducing the pressure on the welfare state — the same death consciousness practiced by Hitler.

A modern-day Herod can even be, strangely enough, a misguided soul of light killing another soul of light.

These modern-day Herods even believe they are doing good for fellow man with a fervor matching the 12th century crusaders as they marched off to the Holy Wars to naively slaughter other souls of light.

This is a strange war.

And for the souls of light who escape the knife in the womb is a well-prepared poisonous diet. A diet of a multitude of additives such as the fluorides used by Hitler in the concentration camps to weaken the will, to destroy the psyche, the mind, the emotional body, and the physical body of the youth, effectively taking them out of circulation.[29] To remove the vitality of the youth is to remove the threat to the Dark Forces' goal of one-world domination and their 1984 Orwellian superstate of a robotized, computerized, controlled population of souls — numbed, anesthetized and dying.

And for the innocent population of the USSR, the Orwellian nightmare of 1984 is here now with each apartment manager directly reporting to the KGB, no citizen free to change jobs or move to another city. Children are encouraged to report on their parents, and a national holiday now commemorates as a hero such a misguided child.[30] All such data and more on each slave-soul inside this superstate is permanently recorded on advanced computers. The technology and computers graciously "donated" by American manufacturers.[31] And the proof of these "philosophies of socialistic equality" is noted in the direction the souls migrate across the borders, and the force it takes to hold them inside. Few crash the Berlin Wall to gain freedom in the East!

"By their fruits ye shall know them,"[32] their romanticized words and prisons of steel.

The forces of darkness are everywhere and are at war with the light. Neither darkness nor light, however, are limited by man-made boundaries. The strategic task for the darkness is simple: remove as quickly as possible from embodiment all souls of light, particularly souls of great light. What better way to do it than by limiting families and by abortions done in sterile hospitals and clinics, with the consent of all?

When Abraham was born in the city of Chaldees, there was a slaughtering of male children to prevent his great light from coming forth to sponsor a great nation. And later, if not for the alertness of Joseph, the flight into Egypt would not have been made, and Jesus would have been beheaded at the hands of Herod's men sent out to kill all male babies to ensure the elimination of the prophesied Messiah. The comings of Krishna and of Moses also tell of violent threats to their incarnations.[33]

This strategy is even better than open war because it can be controlled selectively and in greater numbers. No noise, minimum fuss, mostly silence — at least the cries are not heard—at least not always. The dragon is sly, just waits and waits and so far has an incredible appetite for souls of light and, even before the Supreme Court decision in USA, has taken one-third of the population conceived worldwide.[34]

The Herod Plot is not new or unique, but the effectiveness of this plot cannot be underestimated, and the present scope of it is almost more than a new-age evolving man can comprehend. It is, for the most part, silent, deathly silent.

A Dark Force, utilizing the best tools of modern technology with computers and understanding of mass psychology, has long set their strategy in advance for children of light who may escape Herod's scalpel. To them the war is impersonal and a matter of only personal gain, of stolen light, power and numbers.

Stage II of the dark plan consists of a programmed media: a main diet of television—of more hours per child in a year than are spent in school—completes the cycle through mind control, appetite control, and an over-stimulation of the emotions with a conditioning to violence and sexual stimulation — 1,136 murders-killings-rapes per child viewer per year — and an identification with the spectacular, the violent, and the bizarre.[35] And, of course, television's boring level of culture, somewhat above the caveman with the club, usually depicted as a frustrated, sadistic policeman chasing an idolized criminal, the plot of which is thinly disguised. This says nothing of the strobe-light, syn-chronized effect of television's scan on the physical substance of an impressionable cortex, identified now in research as alpha-wave hypnotic conditioning.[36]

Couple this with a weakening of the school and youth authority and leadership, plus the legalization of marijuana and social acceptance of it in school chil-dren[37] to further deaden the will and motivation and striving on an evolutionary path, and the Dark Forces have just about won the battle, won sadly with the *silent* consent of all.

The final straw is the legal domination of atheism, a 4% minority,[38] over religion in the schools, granting the school the authority to refuse the recognition of God in the form of prayer or meditation because it is considered discriminatory to those who profess to worship atheism.[39] This is the same kind of thinking the Supreme Court used in authorizing abortion, since it would be discrimination against a mother's human will to allow a soul entrapped in her womb freedom to live.

All of this might be described as something man believes he has to accept, which came about gradually, and perhaps each problem in itself seems not so bad.

   We have, then, the searing of American consciousness, as if with a hot iron,[40] to seal and to desensitize it from the plight of our nation,[41] our children, and from the unheard weeping of souls of light, advanced souls ready to volunteer to come to Terra, to offer themselves selflessly, and to assist in her dragging evolution — not without risk and a heavy price to all should their mission fail.

**A Psychoanalyst for
the American Soul
Speaks!**

If a psychoanalyst were to be called in on the case of America's ailing soul at this time, he would have something to say about the self-destructive direction of his patient. Unfortunately, he would also point out in his very first session, if the patient made it to his office, that he didn't think he had much of a patient. His patient was present but didn't seem to recognize that there was much of a problem — only some vague concern that the patient's children were not doing so well. There were some vague threats his country was becoming militarily weak and financially sliding, but since all of these were future problems, they didn't concern him too much. He was more concerned about how to make an overdue payment on his credit card so he could charge a coming ski trip to South America.

The analyst might comment that the patient America doesn't seem to be concerned about what's happening to his own body, his own soul or that of his children, and that he seems hardened and cut off from the world around him, almost blissfully asleep to the potential loss of everything from within and from without, like a cancer cell that takes from the host without giving back, not caring that this attitude and behavior will result in the death of the host and ultimately his own death. But, he says, since he's going to die anyway, he doesn't really much care about the future, so what's the point of the analysis? And the analyst sadly agrees. There is no point in continuing. He'd rather work with someone who can be quickened, who wants to be alive and to understand his place in the order of things.

Should his patient be willing to tarry a moment or two longer, he might even be heard to comment that his patient has developed a cancerous deep hatred of himself that is callously acted out in the destruction of his own offspring.

It would almost appear that his instinct for life and an ever-expanding evolution of his soul has been perverted, turned somehow inward on itself — a spiral of death consciousness — and hypnotized into believing this is all there is. Thus, he is committed to dance his own lonely, selfish death.

The only cure for this hatred is the uncovering of the root of his hatred, the identification of it, and the letting go with forgiveness. He must replace the hatred with a love of himself, recognize the creative power from within, experience reverence for all life as one and, finally, be willing to give his life in service so others can live and evolve, to follow his own etheric pattern and love of life and light.

But his patient is seen staring out the window, having just caught the beat of a punk rock group rising from the street seven stories below.

2.
The Coming of the Avatars

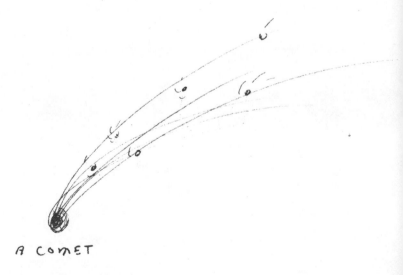

A COMET

And they come…
the Avatars
of this
and
other
worlds
to
Terra
now
known
as
Earth

The Avatars come.

Avatars are advanced souls of great light, of great attainment.

They come bearing a story of a Divine Mission, a story of the birth of Gods, of ordinary Gods of you and I in the womb of time and space, in Mother Earth; the whole story of evolution, of those who have gone on before us, of those who have dedicated their attainment to the goal of freeing us from the cycle of death and rebirth.

They come bearing the story of 2,000 years of testing of those whose hearts are open — who once walked on this planet with a Christ, a Buddha, a Mohammed, a Krishna, a Confucius, who have been the advance volunteers to mission-rescue of Terra from the iron prison, the energy-veil that evil has wrought in the land.

They come with Kohoutek,[1] the light in the sky, of cosmic forces of energy, with the perception of the mark of the beast of Revelation of old.

They come with a story of soul liberation, of karmic law and of dharma, and they come with the divine blueprint for each to discover.

They come with the record of our personal path through the schoolroom we have loved so well on Terra-Earth.

They come with the dawning of the Age of Aquarius, the age of a quickened consciousness, of beauty and a divine freedom.

They come at the close of Jesus' mission of 2,000 years in the Piscean dispensation to prepare the way for the Golden Age, for the presence of angels, of masters, of saints and Buddhas, brothers of light all dressed in auras of white and the many colors of Joseph's coat,[2] to walk with us and talk with us as of old and to herald the secret return of the Christ everywhere.

And they come bearing the word of coming hierarchy — God's government in action as the prophets of old foretold in this time.

"Be of good cheer, O people of earth, for the love of the Cosmic Mother is infinite. Assuming the role of Gabriel, I announce to the people of earth that this day a great number of highly illumined souls are being given birth upon the planet earth. As I AM speaking to you, these beings, who have been in the ante-chamber awaiting their birth upon the planet, are being escorted by glorious Cosmic Beings and angels to the realm of the Maha Chohan to enter the portals of birth. Mothers expectantly awaiting the incoming children shall now receive transcendent souls who shall come forth in the physical octave of Earth to bring joy to all people." —[3]

Lady Master Venus
1962

3.
Life, the Schoolroom of the Soul

Life is a giant schoolroom;
the whole planet the school,
for the souls to learn
mastery and to grow
to become graduate
sons and daughters of
God for greater
creativity and
service
in
the
ever
expanding
cosmic
universe

What is being taught by the experiences of life to souls, young and old — souls in various stages of learning, using this seemingly tired, beat-up old planet as the training ground — is how to evolve toward the consciousness of God, to become more advanced souls with greater increments of light-bearing capacity, for maximum contact with God's universal energy source.

Somehow this fact has escaped man as he continues to grovel in the earth, to scratch out, to eke out his meager existence like the animal life he eats, emulates, and becomes, rather than demonstrating his mastery over everything on earth placed there for him to teach and rule and to raise to a higher, free, evolutionary level.

There has been withheld from him an understanding of cosmic law and the perfect justice of this teacher, a teacher who uses our day to day experiences as examples to illustrate the laws governing the flow of life. No man, no child is capable of learning without some testing, some trial and error. A child overly protected is well-known to become a handicapped, emotionally immature, inefficient adult contributor to society until his early patterning is unlearned.

Every soul in a lifetime is given sufficient opportunity to advance on his path and thereby assist his fellows on the path by example. The path of evolution requires that freedom of choice be protected, since for learning to occur, he must understand the law of cause and effect. Thereby, the return of his deeds — his misused energy — is used to assist him on his path, to learn the price of a wrong choice . . . karma.

The Path of Initiation

Man has not been taught to understand that what he sees with his two eyes and what he touches with his hands is only a single dimension, and that this is only a clue — as above, so below — to a multidimensional universe of experience. He seems unaware that there is an order to things, and the laws of nature, of gravity, are evidence of greater laws of cosmic dimension. This he may begin to understand, when the scales drop from his eyes,[1] as prophesied in the Bible and by prophets in this time at the ending of a cycle of 2,000 years, a millenium.

What is being taught here on earth, in what some have called the "school of hard knocks," is the path of initiation... the testing of the soul. The teacher is everywhere. A failed initiation registers upon the self as confusion, disorientation, irritation and eventually precipitates through the four bodies of man as emotional disorder unrecognized, then finally as maladies of physical dis-ease.

An example is the progress of a stomach ulcer, starting first as mental confusion of the self with others. It then becomes swallowed anger, resentment expressed as repressed emotion. Finally the target organ, the lining of the stomach, starts to disintegrate, evidence of an immediate karmic return, teaching this soul that there has been a failure to handle or master energy.

There is nothing unfair or arbitrary about the return of man's own misused energy. It is only a teacher, and even teachers have limits if the student refuses of his own will to learn. The price, of course, as in the Garden of Eden, is to be cast out of school, to discover what it is like to find a false teacher or to become your own teacher and to go it alone.

The deception of the Dark Force is to make the soul see this experience as punishment. It is not punishment, only a teacher. The student that leaves the school can apply for readmission, and he may be welcomed back, even given a reception, but he will still have to prove his lessons learned.

Reincarnation is simply the return of the soul to earth's schoolroom after a period of reorganization, of rest and recuperation in higher planes. This allows the soul an opportunity to return in another skin, another body, to learn and to pass the initiations necessary for mastery of the physical plane and to balance the misused energy of past lifetimes — to ultimately achieve full soul maturity. And the soul, now no longer bound by the laws of time and space, is a whirling sun of light, a free electron in God's consciousness.

Reincarnation allows further soul advancement when the limits of genetics, of family, of culture, of society, and the physical body itself must be exceeded, and the soul's learning needs must include a different experience.

The Avatars are advanced souls of adept stature that are now also incarnating and using the planet earth's evolutionary platform for their own higher initiations through selfless service for the advancement of earth's evolutions. They come from some of earth's lifewaves of old and also from other advanced systems of worlds, bringing special gifts and talent in all fields, from the spiritual to the scientific.

They come in peace, with light and with humility, and without the confining vibration of materialistic bound evolutions.

You will know them by their light and their works as they mature in their growth cycles approaching 2001.

4.
Spirals of Ascent, Spirals of Descent
Freewill Choice

Cycles turn: "to be or not to be" is the question — to choose the direction of the flow of energy toward light and mastery of time and space or to choose darkness, oblivion and a spiral ending eventually in the death of the soul.

And so each soul or nation learns by choice, by right choice or wrong, this mastery. A combination of millions of right choices results in riding the ascension spiral to complete mastery over planes of matter and time and space, following the same path of Buddha, of Jesus and the saints and adepts of all religions.

The descending spiral is a consistent choice for the self-centered, ego consciousness that seeks pleasure in a material life and a hoarding of the flow of energy. This results in a blocking action of the flow with an increased density registering in the aura as blackness and an equivalent karmic weight that accelerates the gravitational fall of the soul into the death spiral.

In the world of matter-form, consciousness either accelerates and quickens, or decelerates and deadens. There are only two directions. One is toward higher planes and the desire to become the plane of the soul, such as Jonathan Livingston Seagull,[1] with decreased worldly attachment and increased striving for perfection. The other direction is toward identification with material form and the human ego. With the inevitable loss of the body and ego, this latter choice binds man to fear — fear of death.

The aura registers progressively these choices and reflects a vibration of increased density and darkness when the death spiral is the predominate choice.[2] Thought becomes concrete, self-centered and is involved in a world of control and manipulation. Greed, pride, ego adornments cement the attachment to this material world. Pleasure reigns supreme.

Since death is accepted as reality, it is feared. And some souls, to halt the cycles of time, attempt to remain adult-children and often refuse to grow or to carry responsibility.

However, death is often actively courted in an attempt to master the fear, and a cult of death-consciousness with a myriad of sex and death symbols prevail on the planet today with everything from Halloween skeletons to subliminal death skulls in liquor advertising.[3] Then tied to this consciousness is the media's diet of violent death with a heavy dose of sex for seasoning.

The death spiral is programmed into the consciousness from birth onward. Because it teaches death is the end, personal selfishness and selfgetting are the only worthwhile goals. Attachment to possessions, power, love, ego, sex, money, things, persons, places become all-important, and the soul is denied as non-existent, or is just simply ignored.

Death, then, becomes a familiar sweet friend to be avoided by full concentration on the things of the physical plane. And the soul, having consciously cut off the unlimited supply of energy for soul evolution, is left to run on its own battery. The karma builds as density, weight and darkness, and the process accelerates. Such souls are on a descending spiral, and the battery runs down.

The ascending path is a path of searching, of testing, of learning, of discrimination of energy and choice of direction. It is a path of evolution and contact with the hierarchy of light. It is a path of choice for service. It is a selfless path, always searching for greater service. All desire is sacrificed save this one, and the aura and the chakras, now energy centers radiating pure light, reflect this choice. The outer surface, however, may be wrinkled and old from carrying his fellow man's karmic weight, and his face may be stressed and serious. Yet in spite of this burden of karmic weight which is being shared, his countenance reflects joy and bliss in this service.

A problem of the path of light, where the light-bearer carries greater increments of light, rests in the inability of those who are not yet on the path to see light in the aura, until such time when they too step up their conscious-ness. Then the increasing ability to discriminate light from dark will be added to them.

So, the first initiation for the neophyte is an inner heart feeling to try this path with faith and see. For the path is concealed, veiled and hidden until the desire is awakened and quickened by another soul of greater light radiating this energy into a fellow man's receptive electrode — his heart, a cup for light.

There are souls — once of light, but now committed to rebellion and darkness — who are still living out their cycles in time and space, in and out of embodiment. They comprise the force of darkness. They maintain their energy with or without physical bodies on stolen light, stolen from souls of light in embodiment, and by plotting the destruction of a planet for a grand theft of light. They are indeed vampires of the light-energy of the human aura.

Thus, the Dark Force consciously plans to steal this light, this energy, to use as they will, setting elaborate, highly complex methods to engage children of light in their own destruction on an accelerated spiral of death. The motivation for the fallen souls committed to dark-ness is pure hatred and refusal to surrender, out of stubborn pride, to the hierarchy of the light.

The plot highest on the list of the Dark Force is to destroy the freedom of choice by any method, to thereby abort the path of initiation and to seize complete control of the planet.

The coming Avatars seek to expose this downward spiral and to assist in its reversal into the spiral of ascension. As each soul achieves this victory, there is an increased magnetization of other souls to accelerate on the ascending spiral and ultimately for the planet to become a star of great light.

5.
The Law of Karmic Return

Karma is the teacher, using the lesson-book of experience. Karma is just and is mathematically exact. It returns to all impersonally... like the law of gravity. Its impact, however, is felt as if one has been personally singled out. It provides, as an act of kindness, a perfect opportunity to learn by paying back, to balance each overdrawn energy account of misused, misunderstood energy. Through the experience of a measured return of karma, a soul can have the opportunity of a fresh start in another body, to continue on the evolutionary soul path without the handicapping burden of unbalanced karma. For without grace of the teacher's wisdom, the weight of his own overwhelming karma would probably take man right out of embodiment before he could even start the path anew.

Thus are seen souls in incarnation with severe physical handicaps, defects, emotional or mental damage, and man feels a mixture of pity, of sympathy, of horror, of sadness and at times outrage at such an unfeeling God who allows this to happen to such helpless souls. Some souls continue to believe that God is responsible, or irresponsible; and if this is so, maybe He doesn't exist. Western man has not received much help from his teachers. The answers are confusing.

Man has not been taught the law of karma in modern times, especially in the Western world. Once it was taught, but somehow as part of the familiar plot of old, this law of justice and mercy has been systematically, stealthily stolen from his consciousness, page by page, phrase by phrase, until all that's left are the Ten Commandments of Mosaic law that he, with superior knowledge, intellectually "knows" were actually for another time and do not apply now. This type of grand theft is becoming a modus operandi of the Dark Force. "Do the work in silence."

But not all has been stolen. A thief can never quite take all the evidence. And the physical evidence of karmic return is all about us. It only needs to be observed. Much effort has been directed to its removal from Christian teachings and the Bible, and this has almost been successful, but not quite. The teachings of Bhagavad-Gita, of Buddha, of Mohammed, of Krishna, the Essene Gospels, and others all demonstrate this law of fair return as the just teacher. Even in the first book of Christianity, Genesis states, "Whoso sheddeth man's blood, by man shall his blood be shed."[1]

And true to form, the Dark Force, twisting the return of man's karma, demonstrates another strategic plot.

Man is now facing the urgent danger that with the stepping up of the war of Armageddon and the threatening disintegration of mankind, there soon may not be a nation or a free country where the freedom to evolve one's Divine Plan and to exercise free will to balance karma will exist. Without a planetary platform or national platform to balance karma, souls of light will become helplessly entrapped in a materialistic, godless consciousness. They will be unable to extract themselves by the grace of reincarnation, exercising the law of karma, when the platform for this project has been taken from them — stolen by the deception of the Dark Forces. And ironically this too becomes the fair outpicturing of the karmic law, because souls of light have been forewarned by the prophets of today and antiquity that if they fail to respond, they will have to pay back a most expensive debt the hard way — the loss of their own evolutionary base.

Unfortunately, the prophets have also indicated that the loss of this platform could well spell the permanent end of this group of soul lifewaves working out their karma on earth where it was incurred.

So ancient legends go that such an end to certain lifewaves is not a new or unique happening. We have evidence of the loss of the continents of Lemuria and Atlantis on this planet and the recorded history of a great flood. We have as physical evidence of a karmic record, an asteroid belt of floating debris in outer space — traces of a former planet, Hedron, that orbited near the sun of our solar system in ancient times.

The story states that the soul lifewaves working out their karma and evolution on the planet Hedron advanced their materialistic culture to a knowledge of the atomic forces and by misuse of this knowledge destroyed their platform.

Two-thirds of the soul lightwaves of this planet were permanently lost, the remaining one-third were considered by karmic law as still having sufficient "money in their bank," as it were, to be allowed the special opportunity of working their karma out on another planet with other soulwave evolutions.

Once again the story repeated itself and now Maldek, the tenth planet in our solar system, became an asteroid belt. The same soul lightwaves remaining from the second destroyed planet are now present here on Terra to work out their karma. Still, some of these same soul lightwaves have not yet learned and are counted part of the "laggard" souls and dark souls committed to the takeover of earth and its destruction as a platform for evolution. This destruction could result in a godless slave, one-world government or complete planetary dissolution.[2]

The stakes are very high. The plot is not limited to a nation. The plot calls for nothing less than *an abortion of a planet and a people* and the loss of the entire body of soul lightwaves dependent upon this mystery school Terra, once known as Eden.

The Karmic Return to
the Nation

The karmic return to nations has the same meaning. Nations such as Germany that overran Europe in its attempted genocide of the Jewish people have had to pay the price. One result karmically was the splitting of their home soil into two parts, permanently divided. One-half is free, the other half enslaved in a Communist controlled dictatorship with the potential loss of one-half of her souls to darkness.

Lincoln, in his second inaugural address, alluded to the idea that the civil war was the karmic price that had to be paid for the enslaving of a people, and that "the war would have to continue until every drop of blood drawn with the lash shall be paid by another drawn with the sword."[3]

In the alarming spread of world communism, there are clear warnings, and there are the prophetic "voices in the wilderness"[4] that should children of light of the free world allow nation after nation to fall with the enslavement and murder of millions, they will not escape the karmic price for their irresponsibility. Again, Lincoln notes that one-half of the nation cannot be in slavery and the other half free, for a nation so divided will fall — as also will the planet.

Even now in America the continued abortion of the planet and a people has been prophesied to result in weather disturbance, floods, pestilence, plague and food shortage.[5] One can freely associate to the fact that the profuse use of abortion in America is the death of many of the first-born. And a growing statistic reveals that 25% of women aborting their first conception then remain childless, perhaps representing an immediate partial karmic return.[6] There is a biblical reminder that America's karma for her failure to defend the freedom and the blood of the enslaved millions of children of light will result in a karmic return similar to the price of Egypt's going back on her promise to free the Israelites. This failure to keep a divine covenant resulted in plagues, famine, a turning of the waters to blood and the death of her first-born sons.[7] It has been told even this day that waters on the astral plane in America are now turned to blood,[8] and we see here in our own physical plane evidence of increasing contamination to all of our waters.

There is no escape from the return justice of karma. Sometimes it can be postponed by the stepping up of wrong choices, as the Dark Forces are now doing; but it can be held back only so long.

For some souls an unpaid karmic debt could result in the mathematic cancelling out of the soul's identity by the Court of the Sacred Fire, the second death of which Revelation speaks,[9] as the inevitable end result. Since all energy belongs to God, the energy remaining in such recalcitrant souls will be recycled and again utilized by the universal source.

The karmic price will always be paid. Karma is a simple mathematic law of energy.

6.
The Veil of Ignorant Bliss
A Story of Karma

*This is a story
of misunderstanding
and karma.*

*A profile
drawn
from the
archives
of
man*

Also recorded in his scientific journals.[1]

This story is presented from the point of view of a do-gooder — misguided, but very convinced that his social contribution will be ultimately recognized, accepted and rewarded. He is prepared to go through an extended period of being martyred for his high social cause, even completely ignored and passed over if necessary.

John B. is an English chemist, a university graduate, 36 years of age, divorced, has one son living with his ex-wife. He lives alone and does not have much interest in dating. He is the owner of his own chemist's shop, similar to an American drugstore. He owns an expensive sound system in his apartment and is often heard playing Wagnerian operas and other heavy, classical music alone. When not in his shop, he is visiting other various biological laboratories and small, less-known bio-research facilities. His personal interest, population control, was stimulated by three years of military service stationed in India. There he was greatly impressed with what seemed to be India's starving millions — children, old people, animals — all dying in the streets. He noted the peculiar religious customs would not allow well-fed cows to be eaten; meanwhile, humans starved.

All this, coupled with a completely senseless, discriminating caste system that made it a social crime to help someone in need outside of your own caste, greatly angered and confused him. There was just not enough of anything, particularly food, to go around. The government seemed helpless or just ignored the problem.

John, determined to do something about this problem, made a vow on the spot to help the plight of these ignorant people, seemingly helpless in solving their own problems. Upon discharge from the military service, and back home in London, he gained entrance to a chemist school.

Meanwhiile, he devoured everything he could read on research about population control. This problem consumed him.

"It was so simple," he reasoned. "You've got to stop breeding so many people. We do it every day with animals; in fact, by selective breeding of cattle, we can change a cow's milk output in terms of quantity and quality of milk and increase the butterfat content. We can do this even by feeding him less expensive food. As the cow reaches a point of decreasing production, there is no problem about that; the cow will now serve as food for a hungry population.

"In a nation of such ignorant people with so little intellectual potential, you've got to breed the bright ones and let the others die out, or at least reduce their output.

"Since these people are so hopelessly religiously indoctrinated and confused, no attempt to install voluntary population control methods will work. In fact, all attempts have failed. Contraceptives should be made easily available to all of the indigent population. It was no problem with the intelligentsia, they knew better and self-limited their own families; in fact, almost too much.

"The problem is with the inferior masses. Because there is such resistance to education, they just won't learn and won't properly use the free contraceptives to cause a dent in this problem. They are not only ignorant, but are also stubborn in their senseless religious practices. A family of six children, with four starving to the point of only skin on the ribs, will still bring in another child almost automatically. If it were not for the mixed blessing of such a high mortality rate in early infancy, the problem would be worse."

In his studies at the chemist's school he came upon a few of his professors also concerned about this kind of problem who were busy doing private research for large chemical firms to find a chemical solution. They placed him in touch with the Society for the Study of the World's Food Problems. Here he became aware of projected world statistics that indicated that the planet was headed for real trouble by the year 2000.

"At the present birth rate, something must quickly be done to either make more food available or reduce the number of mouths available for consumption."

The more he studied and thought about this problem, the quicker the solutions came.

"They are so obvious, I don't know why I didn't see them before. You just can't let human sympathy get in the way of a social solution. You've got to look at the numbers. The race is not going to get any better unless someone has the courage to take a stand. I never thought Hitler was a good guy, but maybe he had the right idea when it came to breeding a super-race."

Upon graduation from school, he was approached by several members he had known in the Movement for the Benefit of Humanity and asked to join their firm as a promotional sales representative. They were manufacturing birth control pills and because of his experience in India, he was asked to travel there to contact certain businesses that might be able to use their product.

There he again noted the same problems, except this time the Indian government seemed concerned about the problem and certain unofficial representatives discussed with him the possibility of placing a tasteless chemical for birth control in the water supply. Although he did not know too much about this method, he was quite certain he could find the right people to research this problem. He also noted now with some satisfaction that the Indian government was beginning to get tough and was starting to institute punitive sterilization for couples of low financial status that did not heed the

governmental warning about pregnancy. The government was starting to establish a quota system for
pregnancy. This was creating much civil unrest, but he
could see in the long run where this could be successful.
Placing a tasteless contraceptive in the water supply
would be a simpler solution.

Returning to England he had increasing resolve about
his ideas and recognized the government must be
strong in order to bring about immediate change for the
good of all. Here in England they were still sloppy. He
then continued his research and started to encourage
his friends to push for the legalization of abortion as they
now have in India. This was beginning to make a slight
dent in the problem. He recognized this would greatly
help the problem eventually and would be an efficient
way to back up failing contraceptives.

Because of his increasing investment of time and
energy into these ideas and this cause, he had very little
energy left for relating to his wife and child. His wife, an
Anglican by birth, and his one-year old son were
becoming more unhappy, and his wife was threatening
to leave him. He hardly heard her and even thought, as
he looked fondly at his son, that he could see superimposed over his personal feelings one more mouth for the
world to feed, another number, and had moments of
doubt that he should have allowed himself that brief
moment of passion that brought this conception. It was
only a quick mistake, and even though he was usually
careful, his wife didn't seem to mind the error in
judgment. And there it is, another pregnancy. "Too bad I
didn't have the guts to insist on an abortion."

And so it went. Now freed from the trouble of
marriage, he could devote more time to his business. He
continued work as a representative of the chemical firm
and used his savings to purchase a small chemist's shop
on the East side of London.

Working late one evening, John was approached by a man with a peculiar request.

"In your business I'm sure you know a lot of women who want abortions."

John replied, "Yes, but they all go to the state abortion clinic where they can be obtained free. The only ones I see are those who come to me too late to have the state abortions."

The man replied, "These are the ones that we are interested in," and went on to state that his firm was doing some important medical research and would pay £10,000 for every viable fetus they can locate.

"As a man of science, you must know how important it is for medicine and science to use the closest material and specimens that can be obtained that relate to the human body so the research for the benefit of mankind will be valid."

He explained that these specimens were very difficult to locate and that was the reason they were paying such a high price. He casually mentioned that the specimens cannot be obtained from the clinic since they usually do not allow such advanced abortions, such late terminations.

"Unfortunately," he stated, "the laws of the people are slow in evolving and science was greatly handicapped by lack of suitable specimens."

John replied, "Yes, you're quite right," and at that moment, flashing before John's eyes was the appalling scene of death in the streets of India, with flies crawling all over the corpses. He shook the man's hand, took his card, and said he would do what he could to help.

With a renewed sense of determination and hope for the world, and an imperceptible tightening in his chest, he decided to actively participate in this cause.

And the fetuses, through his contact with several of the abortionists (doctors specializing in late terminations), started to flow through his personal delivery service. They had to be handled carefully, like the valuable specimens they were. Packing in ice would slow things down, decreasing blood pressure and skin temperature and would also cut down the squirming and noise.

"It really bothers me when they cry; I almost want to strangle them and run. I get very nervous, but I'm getting better. Just have to remember the cause. They are really just like guinea pigs.

"And the money helps, but it's not the money; it's what the money can do. It's power — I've been donating £5,000 each time to the Foundation for the Benefit of Mankind and they are very grateful people. Not a big organization, yet they are doing a good job of ridding the planet of polio and other chronic diseases. This will help the race.

"Just today, Mr. S. came in and said they have a special request; they need a specimen that is strong enough to last six months. I said sure and asked what for. He said he couldn't reveal this kind of research at this time, but if I wanted to see how they were doing with some of the others, he would see if he could arrange a visit. I thought it would probably be good for me to get over this squeamishness. It would toughen me up for better service for the cause."

And then John B. did become toughened and even found himself looking forward to these visits in a peculiar, strange way. A sense of excitement coursed through his solar plexus about these scientific studies. He liked to go to those laboratories where they work with the living specimens. They were all executed with such precision, such care, such concern for the correct and careful scientific results. Perfect sterility. These men knew what they were doing.

One specimen, a four-month old, was being observed for the effect of certain toxic chemicals when placed directly upon the surface of the human cortex. It had been carefully exposed surgically with a rectangular flap, maintained in a saline solution and the cranial bone removed.[2]

"Amazing research and in a four-month old kid... I mean fetus. Wonder what they do with him later? My friend said they just 'put them down' before they walk.[3] I guess they mean get rid of them. Of course they would. It's done painlessly, a humane thing to do. This is a really professional group of scientists, these men.

"Not like the bucket and the blood of the home-abortion clinics who keep the specimens lying all around, making easy photos the anti-abortionists love to display. It should be stopped. First of all; they will give the profession a bad name. It needs the hand of these kind of professionals. And secondly, it's just plain wasteful to let all this valuable tissue be discarded into garbage. Could be used for making vaccines, organ replacement systems that just can't be obtained now. More live, full-grown specimens would be excellent hosts for the many unknown, severe, fatal, viruses we are seeing more of these days. The specimens could then be sacrificed for the blood and recovery of like viral vaccines for the millions. What a benefit to society!

"In fact, if we would just change the laws a little, look at all the wasted material that is kept in the name of humanity in the retarded homes and the mental incompetents. No one wants them, and society continues to support them for nothing. No society can grow and afford this kind of waste. It's only religious prejudice that keeps the people from taking action for their own good and welfare. Marx was right when he said religion was the opiate of the masses. Religion is the worst, and Lenin states it is the worst sin against the State. I see now why he wanted it eradicated and was ruthless against the religionists. In fact, I can even see what they meant about euthanasia. You've got to work on that problem from both ends to strengthen a society. Get the weak culled out; they can drain the blood of society. Anyone not supporting the state must be eliminated. Killing is mercy, not to be thought of as personal. I will gladly walk to my own death at the age of 80 or 60 with the certainty and knowledge that the state will be stronger."

Exit John B. A soul of some light from the screen of a lifetime on Terra. A misguided soul that led millions of other souls into the darkness and personally contributed to the crucifixion of hundreds of souls of light. All in the name of his own religious idol, science — the idols of which that old karmic schoolbook, the Ten Commandments of the Bible, warn, "Thou shalt have no other gods before me."

The story does not stop here, as John B., in ignorance of the law, had been lead to believe.

One possibility of many:

Thus, John B's soul will be taken in time to an etheric retreat and shown in the flash of a microsecond of no-time his life, his records and results, as well as all past lives. He will weep real tears and will experience real horror and remorse over his misguided actions. And he will be given the opportunity to ask forgiveness and to plead before the Court of the Sacred Fire for another opportunity to live and to return to Terra to undo the damage and to work out his karma.

His request will be solemnly reviewed. The karmic damage, however, is extraordinary. If there is some advanced being who will plead his case based on some evidence that his soul is a salvageable soul who can yet learn by karmic experience, and if he has not exhausted his karmic energy quotient, he may be given another opportunity to return.

Most likely it will requre that he, too, experience a personal abortion or abortions, a crucifixion or crucifixions such as a saline, seven-month abortion, perhaps surviving somehow only to be taken away for a scientific experiment to last until he is able to walk and then "put down" or perhaps to become an abortion of late termination that somehow, against all odds, survives and finds its way as an adopted survivor with all the psychological problems of childhood and adult life — to relearn his error and to pay back the karmic debt.

Whatever the price, his soul knows it will be worth the result that his expanded cosmic vision saw when he was between incarnations.

The case of John B. has a special significance. On one hand, the Court of Sacred Fire will take into account that he initially had a heart center that was partially open, and that the impact of the culture and his university experience were both carefully planned and geared to condition him to a gradual closing of this center, a hardening. The scientific method, his chosen idol, gradually replaced his inner memories of God and the law of hierarchy written in his inner heart. "What one can see, feel, touch, test is the only valid evidence," and gradually he became convinced that it was through the application of these theories only that man could advance himself.

So John B. was innocently deceived, misled. His stand for a cause, even though grossly misguided and in error, was considered courageous by the Karmic Board and an honest mistake and was the one deciding factor in their decision to allow him one more opportunity to return. Because of the great karma he incurred, the balance of this weight had to be held for him by an advanced being who volunteered to sponsor him, or it would not have been possible for him to return. Karmic weight alone would have taken him out of incarnation immediately.

Should he fail in his next incarnation, this advanced being would forfeit the light attainment he had put up as collateral for John.

The law is precise, harmonious and just. Even an advanced being sponsoring a soul in incarnation has a direct connection, an involvement and investment in the outcome. Should John B. succeed in advancing his soul's light attainment, his sponsor will share in this light attainment and pass a higher initiation for himself.

Thus the law works in both directions and is perfect.

7.
Soul Identity, Polarity of the Soul

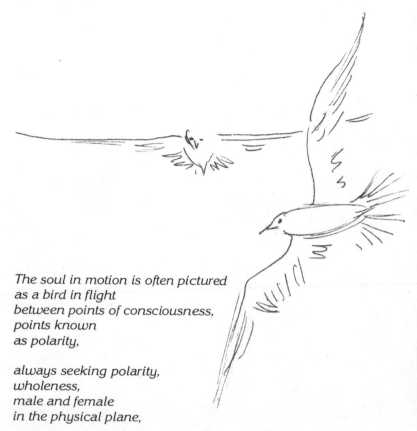

The soul in motion is often pictured
as a bird in flight
between points of consciousness,
points known
as polarity,

always seeking polarity,
wholeness,
male and female
in the physical plane,

briefly uniting in love
to acknowledge oneness,

demonstrating God's transcending,
ever-expanding creativity,

sending forth into motion
another soul,
from above to below.

Within the soul is a pulsing, cycling of energy, of ebbing and flowing, of acting and resting, of thrusting forth and returning, of giving and receiving. When these cycles are in balance, there is a harmony, and energy flows like an undisturbed sound wave over eons of time, returning to us in perfect wave form from the etheric planes of higher consciousness.

"As above so below" is Hermes' ancient law of the universe, a discovery of a grand polarity of spirit and matter, above and below, and the flow between. It can be seen as the flow of souls returning to the realm of Spirit in higher frequency, higher vibrations, and back again from Spirit to the realm of mater, and vice versa.

Each soul in motion reflects the search for balance between spirit and matter.

Unfortunately, man in his present state of evolution, is usually unaware of his search for his soul identity in the outer consciousness and, if questioned, he may even actively deny the existence of the soul and the search, for the soul's vibration is subtle as is also the flow of energy.

And for multiple reasons due to his many layers of karma — density wound around his soul over the centuries — he has so dulled his chakras, his centers for receiving and transmitting these higher vibrations, he is almost unaware he is missing something. But fortunately some signs still remain and this inner search is often reflected in outer pursuits, simple or complex, or in his dreams.

This search may take the form of a search for another soul to become the completeness of himself, or it may be an intuitive recognition that something is missing, undeveloped, or destroyed and must be regained. It is a search for the divine mandala of the Self and seemingly elusive perfection and completeness — wholeness.

This inner search is played out upon the stage of the outer world. A mate is found to be the 'other half;' a career is entered, to become self-realized; friends are made to feel valued. However, man may only discover that that which has been destroyed within is automatically destroyed without, and the search for the outer does not bring peace on the inner. 'All the world is a stage,'[1] and the soul is learning, perhaps slowly, painfully or joyfully, as the case may be.

Thus the inner drama is acted out again and again in the physical, reinforcing old karmic patterns. By the grace of cycles, the karma returns once again for mastery and for the opportunity of the soul to pass another initiation to free itself of karmic weight, allowing him to soar back to the higher planes, free once more from the endless round of death and rebirth.

Inside of each one's consciousness is a masculine and feminine identification, a polarity similar to electrical poles of '+' and '−' and accompanying qualities in various percentages. In man's present state of evolution, this is an approximate balance of 60%/40% male/female characteristics and vice versa for woman.[2] Examined from the viewpoint of the law of magnetic attraction, one could speculate that this would result in a pull to achieve balance in union with a partner of reverse percentages. So, a person of extreme aggressiveness will attract a person of extreme passivity.

The soul of man, evolving toward other planes of consciousness and frequencies beyond the physical plane, will not need physical sexuality as we understand it. He will be gradually lessening his outer need for expression of exaggerated male/female characteristics, and will return to a more balanced male/female ratio and ultimately, in an evolved light body, to 49%/51% in the higher planes of consciousness. However, the greater the off-balance in the soul identity of these percentages of male/female characteristics, the greater will be the pull towards sexual union. And because he has wrapped karmic density about his soul, he may not be able to experience the opening and flow of energy in his higher centers and cannot know the bliss of a communion in the higher planes. In fact, he will not even know of this possibility and will continue his search for a greater orgasm — recognizing only the opening of his sexual energy center and experiencing the flow of his energy as it is drained off through the base of the spine chakra.

We then see in our society today an intense action toward polarization in heterosexual activity, and a seeming violent reaction away from the completeness of the identity of the self, evidenced by confusion at every level, and a stubborn denial of the existence of the soul.

To clarify and understand the confusion of identity
the soul is facing today
we return to the record
of the Beginning
when man was
created by God
made in his
likeness and
was endowed
with his
potential
to become
God
and
to obey
his mandate
to take dominion
over every living thing
and to multiply and replenish the Earth.

FOR THE RECORD: Souls are born out of a single
spirit-spark from the creative hand of God on the inner
planes,
divide into two wholes
a plus and a minus,
then
descend as
masculine
and
feminine
polarities
known
as
twin flames
or
twin souls
to continue
together
their evolution
and
growth,
in
the
schoolroom
known
as
earth.

However, due to the density of earth's physical plane,
souls, rather than minding the business of evolving by
their own free choice, tended to be drawn into misusing
God's energy, and thereby gathered about their soul
sheath karma, as increased density and darkness. Since

each soul half of the twin flames participated unequally in this collection of karmic weight, it prevented twin souls from traveling together on their evolutionary path.

This also caused an unequal balance in the masculine and feminine parts of each individual soul half. By karmic law, before twin flames could again have the opportunity of joining together they would be required to individually achieve wholeness by balancing their masculine and feminine parts — polarities, the father and mother identification within each of their souls.

Thus we see in souls among man a search for another to feel complete, or a deep sense of loneliness which may reflect, even in an advanced soul of solid soul identity, the search for the twin flame and does not necessarily represent a deep imbalance of masculine or feminine polarity. Because of the unequal evolution of souls, twin flames often are not even in embodiment together. If twin souls are fortunate to be in embodiment together, they will be in complimentary sexual identity, male and female.

In man's outer psyche, soul identity is experienced as a sense of completeness, wholeness, a deep inner knowing, and absence of man's usual emotional maladies of anxiety and depression. There is a clarity of direction and purpose. His path is discovered; his work begins. Now firmly set on the path, he knows there is no turning back. He is wedded to his inner vision and there is nothing left for him in the outer world save his one desire to assist others to find the path. His goal is secure. He is as Jesus, "without guile" and nothing was found in him.[3]

In man's inner conscious awareness, the soul identity is more specific. He knows the purpose of his evolution. Across the centuries it has been to discover his soul identity and to reunite again and again with his twin flame to work through the substance of karma for a more rapid evolution. Together, with a greater sense of completeness, they can achieve a more rapid evolution to a perfected identity as a son or daughter of God and then return as the perfected soul brides back to their God Presence in the final ritual of the ascension into the higher planes for greater service.

Unfortunately, many souls among mankind have accumulated so much karma and density that they wander about the face of the earth in the small towns, the cities, even in the uplifting reaches of the mountain top, unaware of the light in their souls . . . and are asleep. They have forgotten who they are, and their light, still visible, is dimmed by the outer bushel of karma surrounding this light.

There are however some souls, perhaps one in one thousand, with a dimmed memory, who are still searching, going here and there — looking for something, but they know not what.

Because of the oncoming wave of light coming to the planet at the ending of this cycle of 2,000 years, souls of light and souls of darkness feel this step up of light energy as a pressure on their being. This increase of light is experienced by man in his chakras.

This light cycles in first to his heart chakra from the universal energy source and then spirals into the base of the spine where it must be raised by free will choice to the higher centers for his evolution.

Most souls in embodiment on the planet have an incomplete soul identity, and do not know what to do with this increased light pressure. Instead of moving the light energy upward — up the kundalini channel — in a balanced figure "8" flow to increase the light in their "lamps," their upper chakras, they seek relief in ignorance from this pressure by draining off the excess energy at the base of the spine with sexual activity of all kinds, drugs, music, etc.

The difficulty is that once, however, light is misqualified — misused as sacred fire — it depletes the soul sheath protection and cannot be easily replaced, and must be paid back in this or another lifetime, perhaps as some emotional illness the price — symptoms of an energy loss.

Basically, this increased pressure of light brings the individual judgment to souls light or dark. They can no longer remain neutral, either they will awaken, become quickened or will use this energy in increased sensual pursuit or pleasure. Spirals of energy will either rise upward as light in the upper chakras and to the causal body of light or will descend as darkness or density in the lower chakras and electronic belt.

When the soul does not have an inner balanced identity of wholeness, it will seek more wholeness on the outer, more sexual union, more partners, and accumulate more karma when these activities are not in harmony with cosmic law.

We see, therefore, in our off-balanced culture today an explosion in sexuality and sexualization of the culture, a new morality, open sexuality, perversions of all kinds openly paraded as normal. We see sexually enhancing drug use such as marijuana which blocks the rise of the kundalini energy up the rod of the spine to the higher centers and thereby increases the pressure on the lower centers causing their rupture and tearing of the protective sheath around the soul ensuring a continual leak of energies. To further augment this loss of energy, rock music composed under this and other drugs is designed to assist in driving the kundalini energy down the spine.

This weakening of the kundalini energy available to the soul results in the syndrome seen often in the chronic marijuana and drug user, a lack of will, a passive attitude, absence of caring for the self or others, a directionless existence, looking for the shortcut without effort and a permanent berth in the welfare state.

In all this great increase of violence, of sexual activity and perversion seeking, these are still souls who are seeking, albeit confused and sand-trapped in search of something but in ignorance of cosmic law and the knowledge of soul evolution.

And so once again enters the Dragon, the Dark Force organized, aware of the oncoming light, yet fearful and agitated, even trembling, at the thought of 10,001 Avatars starting to embody on the planet. And in retaliation, this force of darkness is determined to steal from any and all souls of light their birthright, their soul identity. For without a sealed identity, a soul of light is vulnerable; even an embodying Avatar is vulnerable without protection by soul-aware parents.

And as is by now boringly familiar, but nevertheless effective, the plot is: attack the basic soul identity. The best way to do this is to make sure the souls of light are forced to grow in a programmed culture of sexuality, violence, and moral corruption which will keep the energy drained at the base of the spine and the lower chakras so the kundalini cannot rise in its channel. Or better still, attack and destroy one polarity of the soul. In order for the kundalini to rise, there must be a balance of masculine and feminine energies that interweave about the sides of the kundalini channel.

The Thrust of False Polarity
Homosexuality[4]

So it is no longer a mystery why we suddenly see a great thrust of homosexuality, because it represents for the D.F. a simple formula to hold down the consciousness. When one side of the kundalini is weakened or destroyed, the full thrust of the kundalini, the light energy, cannot rise to the higher centers, and the soul cannot contact its higher identity in wholeness. Without wholeness and balance, the soul cannot achieve its victory by raising the kundalini in the ritual of the ascension.[5]

The repeated misuse of this sacred energy and subsequent damage to the masculine ray in the soul of man or the feminine ray in each soul of woman is carried forward into each succeeding embodiment, and the damage becomes greater as does the karma.

Homosexuality in the male, through the abuse of the masculine energy, attacks and gradually destroys the masculine/father identity, After many embodiments of acting out these hostile energies, the males become very effeminate and childlike in their preoccupation with appearance, recognition, approval, and material desires. They will have mostly hostile, dependent relationships based upon manipulation and a sense of competition with the woman. While not all homosexual males demonstrate these changes overtly, the degeneration of the masculine role is observable in the dream material and free association of the analytic therapy.

And the converse is true, also, of homosexuality in the female, the lesbian. In this case, with the gradual destruction of the female principle, woman begins to lose the faculties of soul sensitivity, of intuitiveness, an inspirational ability, and the more delicate subtle feelings, leaving her more dense, crude, concrete, and masculine-like.

And for the Dark Force backing this social change, not only have they cleverly succeeded in denying souls their evolution, but they also have rejected the potential of sponsoring incoming Avatars — and in one stroke increased the hazard of ensnaring even the Avatars as they mature on earth, to prevent them from completing their mission.

This social change has been put forth through incomplete knowledge and a series of half-truths regarding the homosexual.

The homosexual often believes that his body is

playing tricks on him, that he has the emotions of a woman and that this was some cruel act of the hand of fate, an accident of nature.

Or he is told by a psychic that he actually was supposed to have been a female, and was indeed a female in his past lifetime.

And furthermore, there is some new medical research that seems to be pointing out that homosexuality can be identified at birth chemically.

And recently some well-known psychiatrists have been known to say that homosexuality is a normal human condition and should be taken from the standard medical classification of diseases.

And even some churches are willing to marry homosexual partners and are now allowing their clergy to openly declare their personal sexual preference.

Painfully, the above logic and incomplete information could be accepted, if we did not have the knowledge of the aura, the kundalini, the laws of karma, the path of evolution of the soul, and the war of darkness and light, and the purpose of existence on this planet.

With this expanded knowledge and vision of the greater whole, we quickly see how all of the above parts to the puzzle fit together.

Homosexuality is not what it appears to be on the surface.

In this hypothetical example, the task of the soul, perhaps predominantly a female in a male body — is to learn or relearn karmic lessons. Perhaps the former life was one in which, as a wife, she gravely mistreated her husband and failed to make any soul gain during that life experience, and this may very well be an old pattern, repeated many lifetimes before. So to assist this soul's evolution, it became necessary to experience a male body, albeit handicapped with female characteristics. The special initiation for this soul is to learn not to rebel against the physical body's sexual charge by embracing homosexuality — stubbornly refusing the initiation and increasing the karma. But, in this soul example, the initiation is to learn the lessons of the masculine side of the soul's polarity and to evolve to a greater understanding and true balance of polarity, allowing progress on the path of initiation. A failed initiation is an attempt to halt time and evolution by attempting to return to the polarity of a former lifetime.

Almost without exception, souls entrapped with a homosexual commitment are struggling with childlike relationships. Attempting to control and hold the partner in the relationship, they are almost always involved in child-parent scenes. The partner playing parent conceals even to himself his own fear that this partner-child may leave him, and he, now exposed, also childlike, will be helpless without a parent. So these souls remain embodiment after embodiment — children — fearful of growing up and putting their shoulder to the wheel of life and the community.

Tragically, this rebellion is, in reality, a feeble attempt to reverse the law of karma by denying the present sexual polarity, and denying the law of dharma, to be what you are, erecting a pseudo polarity, homosexuality, in its place. This explains the make-believe masculinity and femininity in the play world of the homosexual. The ultimate acting out of this masquerade is to render permanent in the physical plane a false polarity by transexual surgery.

I have no question that it may be possible to demonstrate corresponding physiological and chemical changes that could be ascribed to an imbalance in the sexual polarity energy system that we may be now observing in the newborn. I might add further that more serious changes may occur as this energy blueprint is karmically damaged.

The emotional pain experienced by the homosexual is simply his personal rebellion against his own karma, and unwillingness to surrender to his soul path.

It has been my experience to observe that most homosexuals require a period of complete sexual abstinance in this lifetime before progress on the evolutionary soul path can be made secure and healing of the damaged side of the kundalini *caduceus* begun. This price, however, for most homosexuals is considered small when the vision of what lies ahead is once seen.

Psychiatry has notoriously a dismal failure rate attempting to change the homosexual's lifestyle without integrating into his psyche an expanded vision. However, psychiatry and psychoanalysis have demonstrated some ability to outwardly relieve the homosexual's deep fear, anxiety, and depression by sympathetically supporting his karma, rather than delving deeper and exposing the cause of the symptom.

The unfortunate position of churches and clergy endorsing homosexuality are caught in exactly the same dynamics as the supportive psychiatrist who use their authority to relieve this deep guilt by covering over the cause of the problem.

And worse yet is the hypnotist who will bury the deep guilt and fear under a layer of greater dependency. And, I might add, may encumber himself personally with the greater karma of damage to the soul of his patient, as will also the clergy supporting homosexuality.

The automatic karmic price for the misuse of the flow of these energies is to perpetuate the return to the physical plane in the same body polarity, only each time with a heavier karma. A known karmic price after lifetimes of misuse of these sacred energies in homosexual indulgence would be a destruction of one side of the caduceus. This could potentially create such a complete off-balance in the soul's energy system that the reconstruction of a perfect mental, emotional or physical body for another embodiment would fail. Painfully, the fair price of learning a very difficult lesson.

Kirlian photography demonstrates the existence of these auric energy blueprints through which energy flows to precipitate physical substance. It also suggests what may happen if an imperfect energy blueprint was brought forward.[6]

Homosexuality also automatically blocks any reunion with a twin flame in the perfect match of polarity, a special union which could accelerate the path of initiation.

Once again the subtle enemy is seen in the all-pervasive war of Armageddon of darkness against the light. If a culture, a race, can be tricked into embracing homosexuality, masquerading as a normal condition, then the individual soul cannot raise his consciousness, since energy cannot flow through the aura with only one pole. Then collectively the aura of the group cannot join together for the multiplication of this light. Energy, light, is short-circuited and a race is grounded out. History has overwhelmingly demonstrated that just before the fall of a society or great culture there has been an increase in sensuality, moral decay, homosexuality, a multiplication of the black arts misusing God's laws of energy, and an infiltration of even the temples of light, the churches, as in Lemuria.[7]

Add to the above equation another part to the plot of the dark ones: the attack on polarity and the flow of energy in the aura. This is disguised under the heading of demanding freedom and equality for women — something with which almost no one can disagree — particularly as we emerge from the suppression of a woman by man during the Victorian culture. The enemy of light is very clever; the innocent, naive children of light are not much of a match for the serpentine, calculating mind of a fallen archangel. In this trumpeting of great freedom for such mislead souls, we see women — souls with female bodies but large percentages of masculine characteristics — following the dark pied piper into rebellion against their own polarity.

Thus, we see emerging from the overvaluing of man, woman's struggle to establish herself a place in this off-balanced world, one that will return to her some dignity and recognition. This has led to some misguided women attempting to free themselves by further devaluing their natural feminine polarity in the perversions of women's liberation. This was done by adopting masculine values and demanding equal recognition, equal pay, equal job opportunity — militantly, aggressively, and with the forcing of false polarities (lesbianism) onto her sexual identity of this lifetime.

For lack of vision of the whole, we observe division, competition, divorce, and the war between sexes internally as well as externally everywhere.

Sadly, the abandoned fruits, the children, are left to inherit this war of Armageddon on the inner and the outer in the form of alienation of their masculine parts from their feminine parts. Now becoming adults, they, too — out of mistaken rebellion — switch sides sexually and continue the battle from the opposite side into homosexuality and lesbianism, increasing their own and the planet's karma.

The Liberation of Women

And America, the perennial supporter of new ideas, appears to have bought the woman's liberation movement and is now experiencing painful second thoughts.

Disguised in the gift of the liberation of woman has been an overt and covert attack on the feminine principles within each soul, male and female.

Psychologically, woman has used a projective defense in her attempt to dispose of her inherited "collective unconscious," a damaged physical self, the internal remains she sees as sacred, dismembered and un-sightly. This projective defense requires that she try to project this damage into her partner, man. Because he also is seen by her, internally and now externally, as the murderer of her feminine parts, he therefore must be similarly punished by her and damaged by stimulation of his guilt, by reverse chauvinism, and be called "a pig," an animal of low estate unworthy of her.

In this strange war, both sides are killing each other. Male and female principles are just about destroyed. These sexual polarities were never meant to be at war with each other or in competition, but are only comple-ments of each other.

Jesus warned women of these times. "Behold the days are coming in which they shall say, blessed are the barren and the wombs that never bore, and the paps which never gave suck."[8] The "liberated" woman is now praised for rejection of her femininity and her childless-ness.

Woman's liberation, in error, believes something has been won! Perhaps she has won some freedom from motherhood and freedom from her feminine polarity. She believes she can now be equal to man, the old idol she internally hates. What confusion! Sadly, the next internal, logical step is to hate herself, then ultimately destroy herself and man together. An ancient civilization that flourished in the Amazon Basin bears record to this old path of sexual warfare, the degeneration of an advanced race and civilization that self-destructed for lack of balanced polarity.[9]

In a peculiar way, women recognize that machines have been a liberating force. Intuitively, she is vaguely aware that with the increase of freedom from physical work she is being given extra time, and she knows that the endless rounds of the suburban housewife catering to three young children is a deathly boredom she wants to avoid.

Senseless coffee klatches of gossip, do-gooder activities, cocktail parties, a heavy diet of television soap operas, chauffering kids to their social events and the parent-teacher meetings, social games at night, and the boredom lifted with an occasional extra-marital affair and, finally, husband leaving with a younger secretary when she is 40 — tired, drained and dead, with the kids on the way out of the house — is not an uplifting spiral.

Women intuitively know that this free time was meant to be used, but they have just not tuned-in to the right vibration.

In the evolving woman who has mastered time and space in the physical plane, such as all of the great saints, Mother Mary, and others not well-recognized by man — Joan of Arc, Kuan Yin, Dr. Maria Montessori, *et al* — there is the mastery of individuality, of leadership and, side by side, the grace and mastery of the feminine polarity without its sacrifice to pseudo-masculine values.

Woman, by first raising up the feminine principle within her, becomes a model for her man — a magnet of inspiration and love that draws up his own descended feminine energy. This returns to him his inspirational, devotional direction damaged since the original fall of Eve in the Garden.

With the dignity of motherhood and the divine feminine principle restored, woman can then assist man in the recovery of his own damaged feminine polarity, so the flow between polarities can be returned to both for the whole and for the continued evolution of the planet.

8.
Marriage, a Soul Initiation

The Merger of Souls as
the Counterbalance of One Another

"Marriage — an unnecessary ritual to create an illusion of security. A piece of paper. A few promises that are a social custom designed more for the convenience of a mechanized society to keep track of the numbers." So goes the dry voice of the intellectual.

And, we add, he is indeed correct when he has no understanding of the light of the soul, of soul evolution, of the human aura, of karmic law and of other planes of consciousness and relates only to the physical plane, what he can see, touch and feel. With the deadening of his consciousness, he cannot even feel vibrational difference, sensations which express evidence of other planes of consciousness.

Souls are attracted, merge, and come together, forging, encircling, enjoining in a greater aura of light for sharing in each other's karmic burden, providing both with assistance on the graduated steps of initiation and evolution. If the attraction has had karmic roots, as in the case of souls harboring anger, hatred, or fear of each other from former lifetimes, they will return to the scene once again to work this problem out and to balance the karma, the misused energies, and to leave in peace rather than create new and additional karma.

Marriage can be and is often used for this kind of karmic replay. What may start out as intense sexual love turns quickly after marriage into hate, the hate and anger it initially was in past lives, and we see quickly following, revulsion, sudden divorce, and a swift increase of karmic debt to once again be worked out in another lifetime.

Marriage is also for a higher purpose. It is for the coming together of two souls in service to assist with each other's evolution in working out their joint life task. It is also to demonstrate God's ever-expanding, creative, transcending Self by providing a protective cradle, a temple for incoming souls of light.

Marriage is a combined forcefield of the energy of two souls. It is designed to assist man in understanding his soul identity through the union with another soul and also to begin the process of moving away from preoccupation with sexual energy by raising their consciousness — spiral together to the higher centers — still, however, in perfect interchange at all levels and in high communion. The sexual center is not meant to be denied or denigrated, but to be understood as a launching platform for the acceleration of the kundalini, the sacred fire. Sacred fire is the energy surrounding the soul and must, therefore, be protected. It is meant to prepare the soul for its ultimate reunion with his individual God-self, God-presence, through the return journey via the higher centers.

Marriage is designed to provide below a microcosmic mystery school experience for souls.

Marriage is for twin souls to form a greater whole, greater than the sum of two parts, forming an aura of light that is often visible on the radiant faces of the bride and groom.

Marriage is meant to be the model below, in the physical plane, for two souls, and for the twin souls to prepare for the highest ritual, the wedding, the union of the soul with the God-presence in spirit above.

Marriage is meant for cosmic union, intercommunion of all four lower bodies.

Marriage as the ritual of conception is discussed in Chapter 10.

**Enjoining of
Twin Flames/Twin Souls**[1]

Twin souls are living flames united. The twin flame is your soul counterpart.

mutually providing each other needs

Born out of a single spirit spark of God, twin flames divide initially into polarities, male and female, each soul whole, destined to assist the other on the path of maturation and evolution. Twin flames were meant to stay together, and a certain number have come together again and again to work out their own karma, and the karma of the planet, in successive embodiments. If separated by karma, as most have been, they may return, if all goes well, near the end of their cycle through time and space, to again join together, forming an auric womb of protection around the incoming souls and to assist in the evolution of the planet.

Twin flames, when in proximity of each other, experience a leaping of flames — visible as a flaring in the etheric. On the outer, there may be a deep inner knowing that this is the one, and may be reflected in the eyes. Because they were destined to be together, the attraction is great and everything may be in order except their karma. Karma collected individually in their lifetimes with others needs balancing and the other twin accelerates and assists in this balancing. Shared karma from former lives together can be experienced as explosive and may drive twin flames apart. When twin flames divorce, heaven may weep — so great is the loss for all souls in the evolutionary chain. However, it is in the fire of the great inner love of the twin flames that this karma and foreign substances may be consumed — karma that has caused such a long separation. This particularly accelerates when the twin flames, using the depth of their knowledge, apply the heat of the transmuting flame to this karmic darkness.

In this communion of love, they also intensify their own alignment and love of God consciousness, which together results in a greater magnetization of their own aura with God that they then can anchor on earth. This results in a more rapid evolution of their own divine plan and those whom they touch. It also assists the new souls they have vowed to sponsor and to protect so they can outpicture soul identification more than the human. Thereby these couples may complete the teachings of Jesus, "greater works than these shall he do, because I go unto my Father,"[2] for God continually transcends himself in an ever-expanding universe of consciousness through the product of His offspring.

Often, however, twin souls do not return together since they have different levels of evolution in points of time and space and one may have achieved enlightenment before the other. In this case, the ascended soul will maintain the perfected vision, the immaculate vision of mastery of time and space, for the other until he or she achieves the victory.

Enjoining of
Soul Mates

Soul mates are souls who have experienced a parallel karmic path and soul evolution. Magnetized by the law of attraction, they carry a common goal, a common dharma to work out together. Once completed, they go on their separate ways. A marriage of soul mates can be a deep experience and a close model of the union of twin flames.

The soul mate contact is characterized by a recognition, a knowing, and there is a reflective quality in all their physical and personality characteristics. They are look-alikes — twins in many respsects, appearance, manner, walk-talk, etc. Personality and physical characteristics of soul mates are not complimentary, as with twin flames, except of course they have sexual polarity.

mutually providing each others needs. That which fills up or completes a thing. see pg 119.

Enjoining of
Two Loving Souls

A marriage of two dedicated souls without twin flame or soul mate status can also approximate the Divine Union and is meant to provide an accelerated environment for soul evolution.

Cosmic Responsibility

Cosmic responsibility is a reward for twin souls and all souls joined in love with the approval of hierarchy. For souls in love whose love is infinite, deep beyond the sexual, spanning all time, radiating as a union in the heart, and bonded with deep respect for the other — this is a union that calls for re-creation. And this re-creation is a cosmic responsibility of twin souls.

When souls of light come together and the coming together is easy, without friction, without sparks, only with flow, this may be a union of twin flames or soul mates. This enjoining is differentiated from the sudden suction of a karmic union of two mis-matched souls drawn together by the unresolved former life experiences which quickly repeats their painful patterns for correction before departing, although some karma can be consumed in this crucible of the love.

The gratitude of twin souls finally rebonded after an eternity of wandering, driven apart by their karma, evolving along separate evolutionary paths is beyond description.

The expression of this gratitude starts a return flow of energy back to the planet that brings forth more evolved perfected souls to the planet to assist it in its evolution and advancement.

These are the families that, because of their mastery and ability to provide an environment for the child free from the internal warring on the inner, have the greatest responsibility to be the cradle for the new souls coming in to raise the planet's evolution. These parents need to recognize the importance of protecting this cradle, since "the greatest union in the universe needs protection and vigilance. It will be tested by the jealous and the lonely."[3]

An initiation failed is to hoard the greater aura of light that twin flames manifest together by selfishly spending it on enjoyment of each other in vacations, hobbies, intellectual pursuits, the building together a fine, childless nest and the rejection of using this opportunity of greater light-energy to work together for the planet and the evolution of its people and, of course, their own.

The physical plane for twin souls was meant only to offer a brief passing for enjoined greater service and re-creation, to work out their divine plan and destiny. The etheric plane for twin souls is reserved for greater union in spirit, and advanced service in bodies of light.

To know in your hearts together that you and yours are twin flames is to also know you stand on the threshold of a grand initiation. It is to know that your separate evolutionary pathways have been fruitful and this final coming together is preparation for the grand initiation of permanently leaving the physical — by mastery together in service this last lifetime.

Wedded together you are a rocket ship,
fueled, readied for flight,
trembling on the launching pad
waiting to ignite...

instantly

now advanced souls with great Light
in another frequency of
God's timeless
universe,
for greater service
in the light.

9.
The Role of Sex in Soul Evolution

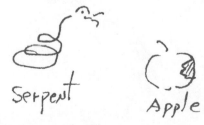

Serpent   Apple

Souls that pass by day in a psychoanalyst's office.

The call of the soul is a small voice. Souls that walk through the psychoanalyst's office are ordinary. Some are in young bodies, young men in their early twenties, and some in their fifties — successful in business and profession, casually but well-dressed. The women that come are usually married, now divorced. They have a child or two, and work in a professional world or other. The men who are married are having an affair or are just over one — the wives unhappy.

The teenagers, boys, failing in school, or almost failing, have no sense of purpose. The girls, fighting with mothers, also failing school — or almost, desire only for mother to buy them another dress. No thought is in their head, except some critical statement made by another girl, or what boy will take them out that night.

The common complaint of all is a sense of drifting, of going nowhere, of not receiving love — or enough of something. There is a sense of dissatisfaction and a mild depression. Sex is mentioned, and sometimes it seems important, but most often it is something automatically expected, like eating. It's missed most often when it's not there, as a regular serving.

Ray is 21, works as an assistant manager of the local bowling alley. He is single, drives a Mustang, lives at home with his mother and an 18 year old brother whose room he shares. Mother, divorced, works as an LVN, on the night shift at Mercy Hospital. Ray has not been an aggressive lad when it comes to knowing about girls. There was almost something shy and reticent acting in him when he thought of talking to a girl, and he recalls today musing in his mind his last date two nights ago.

"I liked the girl and sex was something that one was supposed to have fun about, yet somehow it takes a lot of doing to figure out the patterns and how a guy is to act with a girl. It's awkward, and one just isn't sure of getting it right — then there are all those feelings about the girl, and what if — what will her parents think, and my mother? I wonder if everyone goes through all this, the groping, then the embarrassment, and later all the guys wanting to know how you made out. I just can't tell them what I feel. In fact, I felt uncomfortable and a little guilty, and after all that struggle, it frankly didn't add up to much. I almost wish I were married, it would be easier, but why get married, nobody wants that anymore."

Returning to the old story of the original tempter, we travel light years backwards in time, attempting to help man deal with his basic problems — what he thinks is sexual or real for him. In tracing man's confusion in sexuality, in love, we note the awkwardness, the discomfort, the lack of self-esteem, and the groping of man like the late adolescent trying to make sense of the substance of his ancient inheritance.

From this honest story of a humble, fumbling youth trying to understand himself as a sexual man, we find juxtaposed a fifty year old man, married thirty years, three grown children, and struggling with feelings of feeling sorry for his 48 year old wife. His complaint is that he feels completely void of any desire to approach her sexually, and in moments of weakness believes he doesn't even like her and is bored by her. She is not unattractive for her age and is a person valued in her suburban community. His thoughts drift mostly to his secretary with whom he had an affair about three months ago when he briefly separated from his wife. When not thinking of his secretary, he finds himself caught in a weekly round robin of golf, a game he does not really enjoy. He is not a cold man; in fact, he is quite well-loved as an executive of an L.A. corporation. Because of his long marriage and social life, he does not really wish to divorce his wife. However, he states that he cannot live his life without physical love, it is unthinkable.

These are two souls, separated by a few earth years,
a space of time, unimportant in the potential timeless-
ness of a soul.

They are, unfortunately, typical of many souls who
travel through a psychoanalyst's office, seeking something — thought usually to be happiness, a better sexual
experience, a more giving sexual partner, occasionally a
better job situation — seldom seeking, in their outer
mind, a closer contact with their soul.

Both of these men are typical examples of man
trying to find his place in his battle with life. Nothing has
touched these men, life is just happening. They are
wandering souls. They are vaguely uncomfortable about
one thing in common. The sexual experience is confusing. It does not seem to have any real meaning, nor does
life, although they are hardly aware of this fact.

A psychoanalyst questions in his professional mind —
How did this all come about, man's apathy and his dying
ability to love himself and woman whom he was
supposed to love, engraved by the very physiological
nature of his polarity?

Some thoughts flash foward. One is tempted to
muse of the possibility that the Church was behind this
breakdown in the masculine drive of man. There has
been so much rigidity and dogma in the churches that
man may be burying himself with his guilt. Yet, these
men don't even show guilt, only some apathy.

He wonders. Where have the knights gone? The
aggressive, fun-loving, real men with real swords, real
scars, from real battles? And the women, where are they,
with the grace, softness, and long, silk dresses? And the
men to honor, to love, to cherish, and to worship her
image? And to fight a contest for her kiss? These were
real men and real women — queens and kings — these
Gueneveres and Lancelots. The archetype of man but . . .
gone now!

Something has happened to steal the strength and power from man. These souls today are seen, walking asleep, almost dead, not aware of what is wrong. Any attempt to assist them or to awaken them has no reply — only to talk more about paper gold, or just scoring a game he doesn't care about.

And modern man, caught among the devils as painted, effeminate rock stars, no longer reacts. It is as if he has been sucked dry and become dumb.

And without the assistance of the sensitivity of the feminine energy, he can't become intuitive and aware that his soul is born in spirit and unable to sin, and therefore was always free from original sin.

It is as if there has been a generation of bleeding away of the very vitality, the fire of life of the soul in man, and he is almost used up.

The only goal of life known to these men is that of a sexual pursuit, which we now identify as the counterfeit goal and another plot to destroy the upward flow of man's consciousness and evolution.

The Soul of Man Cut Off

By careful programming of mankind's consciousness — elevating sexual man and sexual woman into false idols and intercourse a grand goal — man has become karmically bound to his false idols. The energy once intended for his upward evolution to the crown center and the etheric plane is now short-circuited to the base of the spine and wasted.

To further ensnare man, he has been sold a misunderstanding that his very conception was a mortal sin. And on schedule, with the false sexual goals enshrined, he then struggles with the burden of a lifetime of sexual guilt.

Buried in man's collective unconscious is the dim memory of the descent of his own intuitive energies, the result of the descent of Eve, woman, which has truly handicapped him from using his own intuitive energies to contact his soul and to recover his lost memory. Part of this memory reflects his birth in spirit and since he is of God, this higher God-free self is without sin.

But man, with his feminine ray blocked, innocent and frustrated, concludes, muttering from the couch, almost tongue in cheek, "Sex must be the villain; had it not been for sex, Eve would not have fallen or tempted Adam." For centuries man has cursed Eve, blamed her for his fall, for his need to earn his bread by the sweat of his brow, to scratch out his meager existence, to fight as the animal with his fellow man for a morsel of food to feed himself and her. And he has been very angry with her and has sought to punish her in many ways, some obvious and many subtle, as the serpent who was the instigator. Sex was identified as the cudgel to punish woman in the disguised name of God's wrath and justice — secretly.

He wonders about the mystery of sex and the Garden of Eden. Can it be so simple as described that man registered so deep a resentment for woman that it has lasted down the centuries of recorded time? Are we still paying a karmic price for her "simple" misdeed — the desire to taste an apple on the Tree of the Knowledge of Good and Evil and listening to the tempter in the form of a false teacher tell her, "Thou shalt not surely die, go ahead and taste it."[1] [This teaches, "Everything is relative, there is no absolute good or evil; only relative good."] "In fact, everything is O.K. There really is no evil," replies the serpentine mind, smiling brightly.

Reaching deeper, the analyst probes the collective unconscious of man and finds the story of Adam and

Eve and the book of Revelation sealed in a code of time
now beginning to open.

The Garden of Eden was simply a protected point in
time and space on the planet where soul evolutions
could work out their karma and divine plans as a
separate human evolution, safely, without mixing into the
karma of other parallel evolutions, such as the animal
evolution.

Eve's mistake in judgment and desire for rapid,
unearned knowledge — the knowledge of good and evil
— became a karmic lesson that returned immediately to
her. What was protected for her, and other souls, in this
etheric mystery school known as Eden, was free will and
freedom of choice, allowing souls to learn and to evolve.
For without free will, souls would simply be rubber-
stamped robots, slaves.

Eve, an advanced daughter of God — by listening to
a false teacher in the garden — failed an intiation of
discrimination — and by accepting his direction to take
of the Tree of Knowledge of Good and Evil,[2] immediately
descended in consciousness, sacrificing much light in
her aura to the false teacher. Her vibration fell to a lower
level frequency, causing her karmically to be naked (her
aura reduced). She was expelled automatically by cosmic law from the protected etheric plane of the Garden
into the physical plane of earth, a plane of lowered
consciousness of relative good and evil, before she had
achieved her mastery and was prepared for this experience.

Because the physical plane also has polarity, male
and female, souls have external sexual differences and
the union of two souls is physical. The bringing forth,
then, of souls into this physical plane will be "in sorrow to
the woman,"[3] which simply means she will experience
birth as the animal evolution in the plane she now shares
— a karmic return to teach her, not as a punishment.

There was no physical sexuality in the mystery school of Eden as we understand in the physical plane of earth. Through the great bond of love between twin flames, new souls were brought forth through an exchange of energy between the highest centers of their light bodies.

Eden was a training school for numbers of advanced souls. They were working closely with their teacher, Maitreya,[4] and were being given graduated initiations in all areas of soul development and growth. The training was intense and complex even though the story filtered through the mass consciousness of man suggests Eden to have been simply a beautiful garden of flowers and unlimited supply, and without responsibility for the children of God living there.

Far from this idyllic-dependent distortion, Eden was not for children of God, but for sons and daughters of God. And the concept of innocence does not reflect innocence as we think of it today. These advanced souls were innocent of sin. They did not have any desire to be apart from their teacher, as they were one — one in heart. They would not know sin, since they were gods,[5] and God cannot look upon evil.[6] They were, however, innocent — unknowledgeable of the ways of the world, and not yet trained to go into dark, dense planes of consciousness. These sons and daughters of God had a mission and these Adams and Eves were to become the leaders, the fathers and mothers, of entire races of light.

The key to their training was in the protection of free will choice. Their judgment had to be honed to a razor sharp edge, so there also had to be a balance within their souls of curiosity — a desire for understanding — against their devotion and love of their teacher, to keep them on the path of growth and evolution.

Eve's curiosity about the Tree of Knowledge was exploited by the penetration of the serpent — a consciousness of the serpentine, twisted logic of Satan.

Her conscious choice, by free will, to go against God, her teacher, was her sin — a direct conscious disobedience. To turn to a false teacher is to go away from God, to leave his aura. This is the only sin possible as a son or daughter of God.

Up to this point, Eve's consciousness was innocent of the knowledge of evil. She could not know any evil and nothing done in this kind of consciousness would be a sin because of the innocence of her consciousness.

And so this was the original sin — separation from the embrace of the teacher, the guru.

Without the embrace — the protection of the aura, the light stepped down to the chela — man is on his own. These are souls who have chosen, by free will choice, to work out their karma and destiny in the density and darkness of earth's physical plane, a plane shared with sons of Belial, sons of darkness, sons that were murderers from the beginning, sons of the liar.

This same temptation is being given to our own children who are exposed to the knowledge of evil in schools and through TV, music, etc., long before their consciousness has attained sufficient attunement with perfection and has the ability to discern rather than to imitate.

When Adam came upon the scene in the Garden and saw Eve's nakedness, he faced a hard choice. He was an advanced son of God and knew the law, as did Eve. He knew karmically that he would have to experience the loss of her in the etheric retreat of Eden. And perhaps because of some incomplete mastery of his level of evolution and the strength of his loyalty to her, for him this was unbearable.

Adam and Eve were twin flames, perfect complements of a greater whole. His love for Eve was very great — great enough to consciously risk sacrificing his soul potential by joining her to assist her in the density of the unknown, lower physical plane, even though he was aware that his leaving to join her was a direct disobedience to his teacher. This is one of the great examples of the depth of love recorded in the very atoms shared by twin flames.

The rest of the story of man is well known: a story of sweat, of cursing the barren soil, of giving birth to souls in pain, and of death and disease. And man over the centuries, cursing Eve for his fall, refused stubbornly to forgive her for her duplicity — her fear of going alone to pay her own karmic price, which would have allowed her to return to the school eventually — and for his own human weakness in listening to her. Instead he projected his own fear of separation into her, then denied it and blamed her for his own free will choice to join her in the physical plane of lowered consciousness, and this has become our inheritance.

Adam, the archetype of man, has failed to understand all these centuries that he made a wrong choice by allowing himself to be seduced by Eve into going with her out of the Garden — a seduction that in no way was sexual. By this action he also failed a higher initiation of twin flames or twin souls. It was his absolute responsibility to remain anchored in the higher plane known as Eden. When Eve left, he could have held the potential of attainment for her, to magnetize and to assist her evolution in his more advanced soul body of light; not to sacrifice his attainment and light to join her, lowering his own consciousness to her level, handicapping his ability to raise her soul consciousness.

And speaking to his patient, the analyst patiently documents a complicated twist of the mind of man... and continues.

A possible psychological interpretation of this story of Eden is that man, as the descendants of Adam, has tried to believe the fiction that this incredible error of judgment was not his mistake. And perhaps his even greater error for centuries has been his practice of the classic psychoanalytic defense of projection of his error by saying it was "woman's fault" and it was that "ole serpent, sex," and both will have to pay for man's karma.

This degradation of woman by projection, condemnation and confusion has cost man the further karmic price of alienating and splitting himself from his evolving soul union out of the Garden with his own twin flame, Eve (woman).

Neither sex nor woman alone are responsible for the fall of man, as man has stubbornly been trying to prove and live out ever since the fall, his fall in consciousness. It has become his shorthand to lump woman and sex and the devil together.

And the analyst sighs... as he continues telling this complicated story — a story made twisted by that old twister of logic so man could not easily escape and would remain confused and dumb.

For man to continue down the ages to put down and attack his feminine side, leaving him more and more handicapped, cut off from the intuitive call of soul — that quiet voice that calls him back to his guru, his teacher — is tragic. Tragic to be self-severed from his own guru who would welcome him home and end his own exile in time.

But the analyst's patients are stubborn — they can't hear him, don't know what he is talking about. "Just help me get out of this situation," they say. "Out of what to what," the analyst replies. "You don't feel anything because you are not sensitive to your feminine creative side," and he continues.

The union with man's own feminine potential was and is absolutely essential in the physical plane to provide man with the balance necessary for both man and woman to achieve the mastery to return in consciousness and vibration to Eden (the Mystery School). This means that this return of feminine energy must be returned to man by woman first in order for both to rise and to evolve.

His fifty year old patient, John, walks out, cheerfully saying, "I won't be in next week — have a golf day; I'm scheduled to play in the tournament."

'But, it's the wrong tournament,' and briefly flashes before the analyst's eyes another tournament with banners, real knights and real ladies, where man knew of the balance beween man and woman and the need to protect these energies for his own soul evolution and the race.

The actors on today's stage just can't understand it's not a sexual joust. The game idea is right but...

But the plot to prevent their return was to ensure that man believed that sex was a sin and thus the cause of his fall. The act of sexual union between two loving souls, even producing the conception of an advanced soul brought into the evolutionary platform of Terra, was to be labeled sinful. From every direction man was to be constantly reminded of his sin: his desire for sex, the object of his desire, woman, with the spectre the "devil" standing close behind as sin personified.

And who wants to lie down with the devil? "Not me," says man, bravely.

And the twister of logic continues to twist and twist. Sex has now become both man's goal and his fear — and the serpent smiles and smiles — helpfully — "go ahead, you can't figure it out — so enjoy it. You might learn something. You will never understand woman. She's on my side anyway."

Perplexed, man then believes if he has a union with his twin soul, Eve, he is in sin and can't raise his consciousness. If he has sinned, he knows he is just as sinful as she and also believes he can't leave her or make it without her. The classic double bind. Since he believes he can't do anything right, he might as well give up and enjoy sex and everything else, since a sinner he is, he's going to die anyway. "Victory for darkness."

Out of this morass of confusion, of double binds, incomplete knowledge, man and woman trying to make sense of their situation, struggling, preoccupied with the task of feeding themselves, have become hardened and bitter. And like the proverbial adolescent, stating in response to the prohibition and the attitude, "You're a sinner no matter," says to himself out of helpless rebellion, "If that's what they think I am, I might as well do it anyway."

And as the analyst probes deeper into the human condition, a change is noted in the souls passing through the door. They seem to be getting more dense. They have almost forgotten who they are, so coated are their souls with dark substance, they can't even remember their original choice. *Sex was not even an issue; just which teacher do you want.*

Thus in this late day we have seen an attempt to free sexuality by certain courageous but misguided souls who found no freedom in condemnation of original sin. So they threw it all overboard and struck out on their own, taking souls with them into open sexuality, promiscuity, with the subsequent backlash of the tail of the dragon detailed by Revelation — of orgies, pornography, promiscuity, aggression and perversions. In this way, they've created further negative auric patterns so complex that few incoming souls of light have been able to escape the karmic burdens which have tied them to a mixture of other lifestreams.

We see again, in the name of relative good, how evil has misguided man's attempt to free himself from the condemnation of original sexual sin, a sin that he intuitively in his heart and soul knows is a lie and a distortion of the old serpent in the Garden. Man has fought this lie, then rebelled against it, only to further ensnarl and entrap himself in a deeper karma.

Coupled with this lie of original sexual sin has been the emotion of deep shame. Shame is a complex emotion that mankind tries to hide from. It is usually connected in man's conscious and unconscious mind as being seen naked, unclothed, and man unconsciously connects being naked as part and parcel of the sexual experience; so once again shame is linked with sex. This is a repressed memory of the collective unconsciousness of man and has nothing to do with sex, but represents the unconscious feeling of being without protection — vulnerability, which is exactly what the memory was for Adam and Eve.

Their pride in their childlike perfection while in the mystery school as favorite sons and daughters of God was their vulnerability. Shame of this failure to be perfect was projected to their sexual parts. Man and woman experience nakedness with an automatic sense of shame and are reminded each time, in the deep unconscious memory, of their failed initiation.

Children, before the age of 12, are given a certain protection — a suspension of their return of karma. Thereby, they do not have the outer memory of the failed initiation until, in a graduated manner, their karma from other embodiments is added to them as they mature, bringing a sense of shame as well as perhaps some emotional illnesses seen around puberty.

Because of the descent into lower consciousness, Adam and Eve associated their loss of light with their failed initiation and their disobedience with their sexuality. Then, as a defensive twist, they buried the memory of the original disobedience into the unconscious where it has persisted as part of the race unconscious of man.

Thus the memory of man's soul identity as God was split from him and his consciousness fixed upon his sexual body as a substitute god. Because man's soul wants to return to his guru-teacher, he keeps trying — trying to reach his teacher through this substitute goal.

He will never get back until he looks up instead of down and understands how he has been duped and that his only sin has been his leaving his teacher. And that can be fixed by rejecting the serpentine path and choosing a straightened path back to the real teacher. *your own christ Self. and your own God self as well as an ascended master.*

10.
Man Transcending Himself

Transcendence — man pulling himself up against the very weight of his collective karma — an impossible task...without cosmic knowledge of the evolution of the soul.

Man transcending himself refers to the creative process for unfolding his soul identity and for the cradling of the new soul during conception and birth.

With faith and courage, man firmly places his foot in the footprints of those gone before on this narrow path, and he finds the desires of the ego begin to fall away. As he walks the path of the self becoming Divine, the sharpness of the path of truth separates him from his accumulated error and unnecessary luggage, his karmic load. It separates the weak-willed from the strong, the wheat from the tares, and parts the veils of maya, of illusion, to lift the scales from his eyes as prophesied in Revelation. Initiates who set their foot on the path to transcend their human consciousness seek the union of the soul with the Divine. The climb is every upward.

Man, when transcended, no longer identifies with his ego — his human creation, human personality, but identifies only with the Divine Ego — his divine creation, his soul. His aura becomes pure white light, able to transmute the karmically darkened aura of other souls and to assist them on the path. He has become a master of cycles, unascended.

Life Begetting Life

The evolving man gives birth to himself over and over. He transcends himself each time, not only in each successive round of death and rebirth, but also often in the step up of cycles in one lifetime. This is endlessly repeated in the microcosm of man in the death and rebirth of millions of new cells within his physical body.

The test of true parenthood is the bringing forth of sons and daughters that will transcend the parents, paralleled in Jesus' own statement to his disciples, "And greater works than these shall ye do because I go unto my father."[1]

So on the eve of the Golden Age, parents are becoming sensitive in the care of all levels of the soul entrusted to them: the physical, emotional, mental and etheric.

The etheric sheath — a forcefield of delicate energy, the protective cradle of the soul — contains the records, memories, imprints and all contacts. Remaining in the unconscious part of the psyche in most individuals, it nevertheless directs and influences action, feeling and thought throughout life. The etheric forcefield in the incoming soul is very vulnerable and impressionable. To sustain this vital forcefield requires the greatest of care, protection and sensitive awareness from both parents for the soul to mature to its full potential.

Conception of the Child

Cycles are considered sacred and have a meaning deeper than the outer mind of man comprehends yet inwardly senses. A mother or father in tune with these inner cycles of the soul seem to sense the presence of soul awaiting in their aura and the time ripe for conception. An opportunity for conception should be offered every month lest parents miss the cycle and must wait for the cycle to come again. They are also intuitively aware of a need to respect the cycle for giving birth. Almost in unison warn the sages and prophets and religious teachers about tampering with cycles. After the decision to conceive, menstrual cycles may vary to correct for the astrological configuration for a new soul. Induced labor for convenience is an aspect of limited mortal consciousness. This interferes with the birth cycles which may short-circuit the full soul potential for this lifetime.

Similar to the age-old urge to clean the house prior to the baby's arrival, the mother experiences a desire to purify the body before conception. If ignored, then the body itself attempts to do the cleaning work with the forced fasting of morning sickness. Chemicals, pills, enzymes from off-balanced emotional states, dense foods, discordant energies — all need to be washed away in preparation for the light that is to enter the mother's body accompanying the new soul. This intensification of her aura becomes an almost visible radiance around the mother, signaling a new soul's presence.

Nine Months

During the nine months of pregnancy, the mother may find the rare pleasure of making inner contact with the spiritual energy of this new earth traveler. As the mother goes within to prepare the hallowed space, the ties, the addictions to the outside world weaken. Desires for drugs, smoking, alcohol, sugar and sex naturally diminish so that the parents-to-be have an opportunity to spend nine months in the peaceful consciousness of abstinence, a willing sacrifice for precipitation of the divine blueprint of the soul into form.

Purification for both parents seriously considering sponsoring a new soul of light intuitively creates an aversion to heavy, dense foods, particularly pork, beef or richly spiced foods. Such a heavy diet of animal flesh presents to the incoming soul the heavier burden of transmuting animal consciousness. Smoking, which absorbs light, acts as a black carbon tar shade at the cellular level of the physical body, presenting an added handicap to conception of the new soul. Alcohol works slightly differently by draining the emotions and consuming light at the cellular level, weakening the parental aura for encircling the new soul they are attempting to welcome. Drugs, marijuana and psychedelics tear the etheric auric sheath and neither the parents-to-be nor the new soul can be adequately protected in such a leaking auric vessel.

Many religious and spiritual teachings advise celibacy, intuitively sensing a need to guard the etheric, spiritual protective sheath around the child during pregnancy. They recognize that premature sexual imprinting may drain the necessary energy he will need to eventually reach a full potential in this lifetime. If the parent's energy is not drained off through the sexual desire body, the energy in the kundalini channel rises and the parents often experience an opening of their heart chakras during pregnancy.

Purity of consciousness has the strongest action in the development of the auric forcefield for the new soul. Meditation on any of the great spiritual teachers, the prophets of all religions, the saints or sages that have walked the way, as well as forms of nature, provides a matrix for perfection of the soul. The free flow of the eyes and the mind as they touch perfect beauty brings the psyche to a state of meditative rest and peace.

The great inspired classic art forms — Michaelangelo, Raphael, Botticelli and many more — and their counterparts in inspirational, classical music — Rachmaninoff, Beethoven, Handel, Mozart, Wagner and others — are thought-forms of divinely inspired perfection and magnetize for the new soul powerful upward spirals of light.[2]

An excellent thoughtform for meditation to assist in the formation and unfolding of your child's perfected blueprint is to hold the awareness of a conception in divine beauty and wholeness. That thoughtform will assist in the formation and unfolding of his perfected blueprint.

**Birth of the Child
in the Physical**

The child's coming is announced by gentle uterine contractions, at times just an ache of the back and it persists. The mother somehow knows this is the time, the cycle is here. This is the first stage of labor. The cervix, the entrance to the womb, starts to expand from the pressure of the child's head.

The second stage starts with stronger, continued contractions reaching finally one minute apart and one minute long and the cervix expands almost to its limit to prepare the birth canal for the passage of the child. Usually during this stage, the pressure causes the protective sack around the child to break and the flood of water announces this fact that the birth is imminent.

The third stage is usually short and represents the final passage of the baby through the birth canal into the waiting arms of the father and assistants.

**Birth of the Child
in Spirit**

The birthing process is the final step in the lowering of the energies of the soul into form. The inner becomes the outer. The heart energies of both father and mother become the focal point for the release and transfer of this energy.

And so begins the process of welcoming the new earth soul.

Soft lights, hushed voices, the flame of votive candles, the waiting warm water bath help subdue the environment. The angels are invited to surround the room and seal it in their auras of white fire. Objects of religious art, which focus the spiritual plane, are used as meditations and light anchors. The father, the nurse, the doctor and all those present are consecrated and blessed, as well as the mother.

The new age mother is prepared in natural childbirth and free from drugs. The need of the hour is to protect the child. The pain only provides the opportunity to master the emotional plane from the consciousness of the heart. As the baby starts its transit through the birth canal, the mother withdraws to deep within, anchors in her heart and stands solidly behind the child. As her awareness switches from herself to the struggle of the child, the spontaneous push through the birth canal walls releases the child as she gains strength in her active inner protective role.

During the third stage, there is that long pause between each contraction, and the mother waits with the child at the threshold of Terra. This last step begins the gentle prodding of the child to venture forth, the image that provides the imprint for continued active support throughout childhood. If the push is too fast, there is a tearing of the tissues, pain and resistance. If the mother pushes too little, the child goes nowhere. And so the mother, with her body as a guide, finds the middle way, that perfect balance that sets the matrix for the years to come to gently guide the child toward his own destiny.

The placing of the child by his father upon his mother's womb is the resting place, a space in the eternity of time. The auras merge and a radiance descends. There is the first breath, the freeing of the umbilical tie, and then submergence in the waters. The placing of the child at the breast begins the eternal flow between the mother and the child, for both to enjoy. Then comes a quiet peace, a time to rest in the auras of awaiting angels.

The now open heart chakras of the parents, if not perverted into fear, form a triangular energy bond between the father, mother, and child — life's great opportunity for both parents to feel the flow of Holy Spirit of the trinity.

Some parents experience that this bond, initiated at the beginning of labor, may last at least forty hours. In this love, the child is sealed for the thirty-three years it will take the soul to mature within the auric protection of the parents.

During these forty mystical hours of sealing the energies of the trinity, the forcefield is a flowing, intense, yet gentle energy of a divine alchemy in process. Father and mother, by maintaining close contact with the new soul, offer the added protection of the trinity. Taking into their bodies only the most simple of juices and waters, and making only the briefest contact with the outside world, the parents may glimpse the world of the soul, a level of consciousness that can give a greater spiritual direction and meaning to their lives. In this unity is a flow of uninterrupted energy encircling their being, a knowing that transcends the ages, an inner peace of their hearts, and a caring, the remembrance of which may help them weather all the initiations that lie ahead.

There is also a special sensitivity to the incoming soul, the joy of reuniting with an old relationship, or the awe of the newness of a beginning relationship. It is the time when the infant's soul is most clearly visible, so often seen as images of an old man or woman on the face of the freshly born.

The Perversion of the Birthing Process

Enlightened parents have mastered the usual discordant elements that accompany many modern hospital births,

designed by well-meaning but insensitive, unknowledgeable persons who know not the vibration of the soul,
but only the physical plane and its limitations.

This mastery has removed the incredible pain, the
terror, the fear, the noise, the glaring lights, the screaming, drugged, out-of-contact mother, unfamiliar hands,
auric-breaking anxious whacks, pain registering on the
face of the infant following an induced forced labor,
metal forceps delivery, followed by an immediate cir-
cumcision without anesthesia. Finally, to ensure the
auric break complete from the mother, there is removal
to a sterile nursery with other screaming infants and
denial of the warm nurture of the breast, followed by
more strange hands. Until all hope seems lost, and the
new soul is already in hell.

With the trinity now broken, baby and father are sent
away, mother is left with the intensity of her energy bond
pulled beyond its limits and is unable to contain her
resulting excitement-anxiety. She is then drugged with
sleeping pills which further reduce her aura. This leaves
the infant child unprotected in his first day in the world
The mother intuitively feels something has been lost,
and it has — the bond of energy with her new soul has
been broken, damaged, unfortunately out of ignorance.

Who dreamed up this procedure where the level of
consciousness was focused only on pain, control of
germs, economic expediency, and convenience without
concern for the psyche and soul? With painful repetition
— just the consciousness of misinformed but good men
— taken in by our old nemesis in disguise, the Plot,
standing by, waiting to devour another soul of light with
another helpful ruse.

It is important for aware parents to develop a sense
of protective discrimination, and carefully select a sensitive doctor to assist at the delivery. Fortunately, some
physicians, as well as some hospitals, are starting to

reshape the environment of the delivery rooms and are willing to work with parents that have this need to protect the incoming souls. Even a few doctors will now work with mothers desiring a home delivery.

Protecting the Aura
of the Child — The First Three Months

The aura, like the vulnerable soft spot at the crown of the newly born, is very impressionable and malleable during the first three months. Everything and everyone that the child's aura contacts leaves an imprint of karmic patterns which eventually becomes part of the soul's outer personality.

Protecting the new soul from loud noises, irregular rhythm, television, emotional disruptions are all part of a deep parental instinct. Many mothers intuitively recoil from outsiders touching the child and their intuitition is correct. For the aura of the new child during the first three months is malleable, and his light can be easily drained in exchange for the lower vibrations of some adults.

The use of natural fibers, of wooden toys, transfer to the aura of the new child a symmetrical cellular atomic structure instead of the chaotic, man-combined irregular molecular form patterning of the synthetic substances, easily observed in an electron microscope. Infants are most in tune with delicate pastels. Red and black are to be avoided. Delicate pastels are closest to the many shadings of colors the child has known at inner levels. All colors emit vibrations which are perceived in the aura of the infant.

Toys must be carefully selected as their images have the same potential for imprinting. Avoid animal toys during the first three months, since they will imprint the animal consciousness. They can be added later when the etheric, higher consciousness has been set.

Tapes of classical music, waltzes, hymns, religious music, Christmas music, chantings or prayers provide a protective forcefield for the new soul. Within this energy the soul can grow in peace, be nurtured, and identify with the higher planes.

The handling by siblings is minimized, especially when they are in a jealous state, and even by parents when they are upset. Crowds are to be avoided, with their large forcefields of mixed, confused, heavy energy. Even visitors influence the aura and may upset the protective energy in the home. If the forcefield is shattered, it can be rebalanced by prayer, chanting, and certain types of high, classical music.

In the ritual of nursing, milk carries energy between the mother and the child. This becomes, perhaps, nature's way of balancing and healing the aura each day. The breasts form two poles of a figure "8" pattern of energy flow of the yin and yang, of masculine-feminine polarities crossing at the heart center. This flow enhances the opening of the heart center so important for the protection of the child in these first three months.

The key in raising a child is to keep all forces in balance — the middle way of the Buddha. Thus, the baby needs to nurse from both breasts at each feeding to hold this balance. The time and place of nursing must be protected. It provides a rare opportunity for the mother to feel her own Divine Presence merging with that of her child's within the radiance of her expanded and opened heart chakra. A special bond evolves between mother and child at the breast. We suspect there may be a protein carrier of patterning that the infant takes into his physical body via mother's milk that is more than an immunological protection.[3]

Introducing the Child
to the World

Over the childhood years, the involvement of the parents comes to a gradual end, culminating in the child psychologically taking into his own aura, his own psyche, a set of protecting, loving parents. This pair of internalized parents serves him throughout his lifetime. This specific patterning is necessary to prevent developing an overdependent personality and becomes the bulwark for his evolutionary platform.

The child needs to receive the world, its people, texture, foods, sensations in small amounts first. Babies are particularly sensitive and may fuss, cry, or even scream when people with disturbed vibrational states come into their aura.

There is a uniqueness in each child's patterning. The colicky child may require purer food and more support while he is learning to experience pain. The allergic child — a higher vibration, a cleaner environment; the slow, gentle child — an environment in tune with the delicateness of nature; the hyperactive child — a protective environment where he can have space to both express and limit the intensity of his nature; the handicapped child — a respect and special training for developing the qualities necessary to overcome the burden his soul has agreed to carry in this lifetime, either for himself karmically or for mankind.

The keynote responsibility of the parent is to trust, to intuit, and to understand the uniqueness of each child so that he can be protected, directed, taught and brought to blossom for setting the course of the coming Golden Age.

11.
The Raising of the Planet

As man nears the end of the 2,000 year cycle of the Piscean Age and final chapter of the book of Revelation, he sees more clearly the light and the dark shadow.

On the dark side, there is the smoke, the pall, and the toll of death to all souls coming to this besieged planet. In America, this death is barely recorded in America's conscience. She cannot look at it or see it, nor does she want to look at her own decline into darkness.

America's forefathers began by forging in spiritual fire the task of bringing into the physical plane constitutional constructs for the creation of this nation as a reflection of Divine Law. Man has seen this nation become fruitful and multiply unlike any other on Terra as the proof of her attunement with a higher and more expansive energy. Yet as the laws become qualified, erased, and controlled beyond recognition, and the letter of the law takes precedence over the principle of the law, he finds now compromise rather than leadership, apathy rather than creativity, polite surrender rather than standing firm to those who have been the murderers of the children and teachers of God. America and an evolution is on the decline. One-third of the nation idle and dependent.[1] One-eighth of the youth leaving school.[2] The economic and defensive systems breaking down, and one-half of wealth is spent in taxes to sustain an ever-expanding government.[3] Treaties are broken at the whim of an arrogant government, and alliances are made with enemies of freedom and God.

On the side of light there is yet hope through the hint of a new resurgence of spiritual energy flowing through the clogged arteries and veins of America today. One-third of America has quietly reaffirmed their belief in Christianity.[4] Ninety-six percent of America believe in the overshadowing presence of God in His many manifestations,[5] and in this final hour, they are awakening just in time to welcome incoming souls of great light and to reverse the declining birth rate of 1.6 children per family in America today,[6] an all-time low.

If each dedicated family could become part of cosmic history by bringing in at least one more soul to raise up the House of Amerca, the foundation stone for the new planet, the power of darkness can be reversed.

This power of darkness is pervasive everywhere on the planet. And the greatest outer threat to the evolutionary platform is the teaching of socialism expressed in the Communist Manifesto and all its hydra-headed manifestations.

Bonding together the very bricks of the Communist Manifesto is the mortar of hatred — hatred of light and the vow of not resting until the socialist dictatorship of the Proletariat is established everywhere on the planet. To stamp this socialist dictatorship on the face of man, any means to achieve this end, including the copious use of sheer terror is justified. This Manifesto of darkness called for the elimination of all private property, the dissolution of the family unit, and the destruction of what Lenin called the "opiate of the people," religion.

The Fatima Prophecy [7]

In 1917, at the exact moment the Bolschevic revolutionary army entered a church in Moscow and killed those in prayer — mothers, fathers, and children — Mother Mary appeared to three young children in Portugal. She gave to these special children the Fatima Prophecy. The Prophecy predicted World War II, the Asian wars (Viet Nam, Cambodia), the infiltration of Communism in the Roman Catholic Church of Italy, and the war at the end of the century "to make oceans boil." The Prophecy emphasized that these predictions were unavoidable unless Communism was stopped.

However, the Prophecy also stated that Communism could be stopped by souls of light consecrating Russia and the energy of her people to the Immaculate Heart of Mary in the meditation of the Rosary, and for each soul in freedom to arc their heart with a soul of light in Russia to allow for the revolution of light to penetrate the Iron Curtain.

This revolution of light is expected to start first in America and spread to all nations. It is to be a revolution of higher consciousness, a revolution to reverse the destruction of America from within and without, a revolution to restore divine purpose to the armed forces, to the scientists, to the Congress, and to all those in the forefront of the defense of America.

12.
The Turning of Cycles
The Oncoming Wave of Light

The cycles turn and an intense energy wave of light is oncoming to the planet, ready or not. These vibrations of increased light are already felt by sensitive souls and are confirmed by the quaking of darkness as the battle of Armageddon is stepped up.

If enough souls recognize their mission in time to transcend their human creation and to give birth to their cosmic consciousness for mastery in this physical plane, then and only then can the return of mankind's accumulated karma be withstood and transmuted — this karmic energy transformed by each sensitive soul becoming a mighty step-down transformer, an electrode for holding the light of this incredible return current of God's cyclic energy.

If there are not enough mature souls among mankind — masters of light in incarnation — the hand of the return of man's karma cannot be withstood, or the energy balanced. Then a great darkness as prophesied will overtake civilization and the planet. For millions of souls, this darkness may be the loss of a final opportunity to ride this giant cycling wave of light to victory.

Souls surviving, but engulfed in this darkness, will call, as prophesied, for the mountains to "fall on us"[1] — so great will be this darkness. If man does not succeed, civilizaton as we know it now will regress to perhaps the level of primordial man. Man, self-judged and now handicapped karmically with a primitive, unevolved physical form and psyche, must once again scratch his way up the evolutionary ladder, repeating his own painful history when he and thousands of others along with Adam and Eve were cast out of Eden.

To arrest this darkness, there is coming to America and the planet an endowed consciousness of spirit as one by one the true sons and daughters of God rise to their lawful inheritance and take command of this land, and this nation born to be free.

The call rings forth! The call commands! The call dares kindred souls of light to "come and see" and "become a separate and chosen people,"[2] apart from the self-centered, materialistic death consciousness of a dying planet. The call goes out to those who read and know this message. For the abortion of this nation, this planet and its people must be reversed by the men and women who have not the mark of the beast imprinted on their forehead and who joyfully proclaim liberation for souls of light and volunteer to sponsor the waiting millions of potential Christed children, souls whose mission is to bring in the Golden Age.

And among enlightened parents there must be found those 'Josephs and Marys' with courage to step forward and to cradle the 10,001 — 10,001 living electrodes of fire.

Test this work in your heart. If this knowledge seems false — release it. If you do not understand, set it aside for a later time. But if this work be true for you, then send it forth from the living fire in your heart to ignite . . .

to ignite
ANOTHER HEART
A PLANET AND A PEOPLE
A GOLDEN AGE OF LIGHT.

Part III

The Prophecy Incarnate

In all cycles of time known and recorded by man, and in those not recorded by man but permanently recorded in the etheric records known as akasha, have been wise men, sages, saints and prophets. Because of their more advanced consciousness, they were more in tune with the hierarchy of God's government and, therefore to them fell the awesome task of informing less advanced souls and brothers of the light of the state of their declining affairs, as related to the impending return of overdue karma. These have never been popular persons for their obviously unwelcome news. And most have utlimately gone the route of the crucifixion for their perplexing sacrificial willingneses to speak the word of God — the Word made flesh, the Word incarnate — to a stubborn audience.

The Upanishads, the Koran, and the Bhagavad-Gita are among many collections of the Sacred Word. And the Bible is one of the major sources of the Word dictated over time, dictated to many individual trusted souls. Before and after there have been also other souls of light that have incarnated the Word through dictations in every age and land to the present time.

Since 1958 there have been two trusted souls in embodiment in America commissioned by hierarchy to continue this unbroken chain of the prophets with God's hierarchy,[1] Mark L. Prophet and later his wife Elizabeth Clare Prophet who assumed his mantle when he was called directly by hierarchy to serve in the planes of spirit. These are the two witnesses spoken of in the book of Revelation.

A dictation is taken by such a pretrained advanced soul directly during meditation by the overshadowing of one of God's representatives, using the vehicle of the four bodies of the messenger to express His consciousness. The messenger remains fully conscious during the message. She is not in a trance and uses no psychic methods or props, offering only her emptied, purified consciousness as a crystal cup for God's representative to use.

The dictations are taped on the spot and transcribed for your study. The ascended beings communicate their message and information directly to souls on this planet to assist in a more rapid evolution of light. They insist that each phrase, each sentence, each single word be tested in your heart for the accuracy of this knowledge.

The following dictations were collected together at the request of these ascended beings of light to be presented to the planet, and specifically to America, for her own enlightenment and free will choice on this general subject of "abortion of a planet and a people" and the impending karmic return.

The dictations are printed verbatim as they were received and taped...

You're on your own
recognizance...
with love
from
the
Mother of the World.

Dictations

Mother Mary

A Letter — July 1972

To the Freeborn and Those Who Would Be:

Each day many among mankind awaken from their sleep plagued with uncertainty. Their concerns extend to the Christian church, to their nation, to their children and members of their society. They fear what is coming upon earth. Is the population of the world increasing too rapidly or too slowly? Why is there such tremendous violence upon the planetary body?

Why, in this beautiful world that can be filled with the hope of the Divine Mother and the carefree attitude of the holy innocents which many have experienced in childhood, do sophisticated mankind fail to comprehend the meaning of life's experiences? Let it be made clear that human struggle is the result of humanity's selfishness, of their failure to appropriate the divine abundance and to apprehend the universal purpose. Seeing life then in its smallest dimensions, they are not able to grasp the perspective of the overall picture; for they have already circumscribed the potential of their life with their own sense of limitation.

Human struggle result of selfishness

Long before there was a compendium of the
Law known as the Christian Bible, combining the
ancient writings of the prophets of Israel with the followers of Christ who set forth the New Testament,
there existed at the time of Enoch prior to the Flood
mere fragments of what could be called a sacred

Bible of nature
  recorded in atoms of
  earth

scripture. Yet the bible of nature, the recording of
the Law in engrams of Light, was then and has always been present within the very atoms of the earth
itself. Just as man today does not build without a
blueprint, so Cosmos was designed after that
universal perfection which God was from the
beginning and is forever.

Don't you see then, inasmuch as perfection is
ever the divine lot, how easy it would have been had
mankind chosen to walk within the confines of the
Great Law to perpetuate perfection throughout the
world? Yet in the dispensation of free will as it is held

Chastening

by embodied mankind today, there is a chastening
that comes from man's inherent freedom to create
imperfectly and to live in error. Among the errors

Errors of dogma

which mankind have perpetuated are errors of
dogma adhered to by countless individuals who are
the blind leading the blind that all mankind may fall
into the ditch.

Now there has come before the Karmic Lords
the question of what shall be done about modern

Man's violations of
  cosmic law

man and his behavior patterns, his violations of
cosmic law, the torment he has inflicted upon nature and upon his fellowmen. All of Life is offended,
and that mortally so, beloved ones. Whereas the
Karmic Board and the hosts of heaven have sought
to stave off the karmic recompense which should
long ago have been loosed upon mankind, they
have persistently held back the onslaught of the
world's misqualified energies in the fond hope that
the terrible inhumanities practiced against God and
man by the people of the earth would cease and the
trend toward more and more evil be checked.

Men are prone to believe in a personal savior —
one who can deliver them from their sins as well as
from those circumstances which cause them pain

and suffering. Then there is the tendency toward radicalism, which engenders human hatred against those who either in politics or religion are not as radical as the radicals think they ought to be. There is

Spiritual pride

human self-righteousness and spiritual pride that has become a terrible weight swung upon the thread of mankind's oppressive sense of foreboding and the desire to inflict punishment upon one another. This has caused untold sorrow in spiritual realms as well as hardship upon earth. Like a sword of Damocles, humanity's damning indictments of one another's faith in God and in Christ hang over their heads as an indictment of their own sinful consciousness, while their challenges of the universality of divine purpose and the beauty of the pure in heart continue to reinforce the brutal walls mankind have erected among themselves.

I, who sought so often and so earnestly in past lives as well as during my embodiment as the mother of Jesus to be a peacemaker, have much to give to those who would pour oil upon the troubled waters of mankind's consciousness. Contrary to the

Apostles squabbled

opinions of some, the early disciples and apostles often squabbled as do disciples of Christ today. It was no easy task to show them the error of their ways and to place in perspective the little concerns that they so frequently voiced, which were not nearly as important as the state of the altar of being, the chalice of the heart, and mankind's attunement with the purposes of God.

Men have often strained at a gnat and swallowed a camel; and how they still need with all their getting, even of things spiritual, to get understanding and compassion. It is not enough for men to be bold in their search for Truth; for all require that bountiful humility which, like a great magnet of cosmic love, draws the love of God through the whole net and fiber of creation, infusing it with the glow of cosmic intent and true spiritual compassion.

My numerous
appearances

Why is it that from time to time in my numerous appearances to many among the faithful, as at

Fatima, Garabandal to
warn

Self-righteousness
a barrier

One cosmic purpose
Merging of flames,
God and man

Fatima and Garabandal, I have often sought to warn? It is because in reality in mankind's free will there is an element of divine grace which can be called into action, a focus of great love and understanding that can remove the hardness of heart with which mankind have so frequently cloaked their activities. Sometimes it appears to us as though man does not really understand the power that God wields. In the universal, macrocosmic sense, the all-power of God is the "all power in heaven and in earth" which is given to those who attain Christmastery and their joint heirship with God through the reality of the Universal Son.

What a pity it is that self-righteousness is such a barrier to divine Reality and to the teachings of the Holy Spirit. For the Holy Spirit guides all men into all Truth. And Truth, beloved mankind, is not just the letter of the Law as it is interpreted by various groups, which may well differ in their comprehension of sacred scripture and still be composed of hearts that truly seek the Light. To have love without the illumination of the Christ Mind and the power to rightly divide the Word is often not enough to promote the universal righteousness of God-activity within the consciousness of the individual that brings divine justice to all.

That the perfect balance of the Holy Trinity may permeate the consciousness of the true followers of God is our prayer. For truly the will of God that is above ought to be done below. But as long as men allow themselves to be hung on the various pegs of their human concepts — or even those of their divine concepts as they understand them — when those concepts are not rightly divided by the Spirit, so long will they remain in separate camps. In reality there is one cosmic purpose; and that purpose, which is the ultimate merging of the flames of God and man, will one day reveal itself to all by the Light of the one Spirit.

I call for your consideration of these matters, even in an elementary way. For if thought will not provide easement to humanity's struggles, then

Pray with me
Christian world
  stripped of hardness
  of heart

Darkness be overcome

prayer will. Therefore I urge all to pray with me and with the Masters of Light and Love that the Christian world be stripped of the elements of hardness of heart and cruelty to those it regards as nonbelievers or heretics, of its shouting-forth of charge and countercharge, of its sense of struggle that is like the thrashing of a dying animal.

Truly darkness shall be overcome, but it shall ever be overcome by Light. For darkness cannot overcome itself. And when the Light is misqualified by darkness, its fruit cannot bring about a Christ-victory either for humanity or for the little monad of self. We await that greater understanding which descends upon the world as a giant curtain of Light and enfolds the hearts of those who would follow God as dear children.

Devotedly I remain,
Mary

Maitreya

October 1973

All of heaven is ablaze with God tonight, for the heavens rejoice to declare the glory of the Lord that descends into form. The praise of Christmas angels announcing the birth of the Christ Child is heard in every human heart and in every divine heart made permanent in God's Heart.

I AM the Consciousness of the Cosmic Christ. And in the center of the sphere of Being I AM! And from that point I project out in all directions the awareness of God as Christ, as the Word Incarnate! Where I AM, I AM the precipitation — as above, so below — of the Light from far-off worlds; for to be in the center of Cosmic Christ Consciousness is to be aware simultaneously with the incarnation of the Christ.

There is a Light that is in the sun that is yearning to manifest upon earth. There is a Light that shall indeed come forth where souls are prepared to receive that Light. And thus the reward for service is more service. To those who have shown themselves worthy of bringing forth the Christ, to these is opportunity renewed every hour, every year, every day. And

Announce birth of Christ Child in every heart

Word Incarnate

Those worthy of bringing forth the Christ

Heaven looks first to
you

thus Heaven looks first to you — to the Mother of the
Flame, to the Holy Family, to the Community of the
Holy Spirit — to impart the most holy offering of av-
atars descending.

Opportunity to bring
forth the Christed
Children

Before your free will, before your souls this
night do the angels of record and angels of the Lord
read the proclamation "Opportunity to Bring Forth
Christed Children." And thus, not bypassing the
Mother of the Flame and including all, the Lords of
Karma give to you, one and all, the opportunity to
elect to bring forth the Son of God. And if you by
your free will shall determine to bypass the opportunity, then, as in the parable [see Matt. 22:1-14], our
angels will go forth into the highways and byways of
life, there to find those who are ready and willing to
come to the marriage feast.

Frequencies of minds

Precious hearts, there is no question as we
mark the decibels, the frequencies, of minds con-
tacting the Mind of the Cosmic Christ, that the
greater majority of souls who are daily accomplish-
ing this attunement is among the Keepers of the
Flame and the followers of the Ascended Master
teachings the world around. This is not prejudice;
this is not a lack of perspective: it is simply fact. And
as you gaze with inner eye from inner realms, you

Window of the soul

can also see through the window of the soul how the
manifestation of the Light is quickened in those
who declare, "I AM that I AM..."

And therefore, opportunity is given for you to
elect to present yourselves a living sacrifice unto the
Lord God Almighty. And to you I make known this

Comet of the century to
foretell the birth of
many Christed ones

hour that the comet of the century comes to foretell
the birth of many Christed ones, many souls who
are to descend within the coming twelvemonth.
And thus because preparations must be made, we
shall not tarry in our announcement of this dispensation. For those who would apply and receive the
seal of our approval and our blessing must do so

Provide the cradle and
crucible

speedily, that time and space might provide the cradle and the crucible for incoming souls.

Let your life, your very being, your very consciousness, provide the nexus for the descent of

Light-bearers. The nexus is the place in the hourglass where the sand falls grain by grain. The Christ is the nexus of man's being, as the Mediator, the Christed One, stands between God and man. Your own Christed Being, therefore, is the Mediator whereby you may receive into your being and consciousness souls of Light hallowed, waiting to come forth.

And I desire that this my message to you this night shall be published abroad in the **Summit Beacon** so that all who are watching and waiting for the Word of the Lord might have equal opportunity to respond to the marriage feast, to offer home and hearth for precious souls of Light. The heavens declare the glory of the Lord! The earth receiveth the glory of the Lord! In giving and receiving, Life is born anew. And the rebirth of sacred spirals, of stars descending, winding in spirals of crystal fire mist, comes now as blessing and as the justice meted out to those who have given, not that they might receive, and therefore they shall receive.

Into the waiting cup of each consciousness uplifted there comes the dewdrop rare, the fragrance of angel prayer. And angel wings, gentle and soft, carry souls aloft into the air, into the sky. And thus as mankind rise, angels descend; and there is that holy rapture of meeting the Son of God in the air. And man ascends and God descends! And then that place, the six-pointed Star of Being becomes the Star of Bethlehem marking the place where a God is born, where a Christ is born.

I AM the Initiator, testing you in the hour of victory. Shirk not responsibility. Shrink not from testing, but proclaim the Sacred Law! With rejoicing go forth to meet the challenge of fire at the eleventh hour of each day, of each year, of each cycle of fulfillment. For there I stand to welcome you, to offer you the opportunity to seal and make permanent the victory of a cycle. And this is a testing that must come to seal all other testings of all other hierarchies each step of the way.

Respond to the
marriage feast

Sacred spirals stars
descending crystal
fire mist

Six-pointed star

I AM the initiator

I welcome you
I offer opportunity
Seal the victory

Shiva

March 1978

Let light penetrate to the center of the flame. Let light as the action of the sacred fire now imbue the soul with *Shiva!* I AM come. You have called. Now let us discover what oneness with *Shiva!* can mean for the victory.

By the lightning of love from the Great Central Sun, this *is* the age of the Holy Spirit and I AM *Shiva!* Now let the company of devas, let the company of angels come forth. So the Lords of Flame have sent the flaming ones for the age of the discovery of the Self in love. By the action of love that you have called forth, I am determined to place within the earth

rods of the energy of the sacred fire whereby those fallen ones who have come out of the pit to desecrate life shall be bound.

Beloved ones, the earth is rampant with unclean spirits that hover and that move. Beloved ones, these fallen ones have invaded the very temples of the light-bearers through the misuse of energy and rhythm. You have been told again and again and yet I say it again: that which has perverted life has come through the misuse of the rhythm of the white-fire core. It steals into the subconscious mind by the abuse of the body.

Alcohol, drugs, sugar

Fibers of spiritual body

Rock music

Rebellions against love
— perverted sound

Perversion of sound
caused sinking of
Lemuria, Atlantis

Misuse of the science

The presence of sugar, alcohol, nicotine, drugs of every description and kind within the temple are a weakening of the very fibers of the spiritual body whereby that body can contain light — all of this aggravated by the rhythm of that rock music and the acid rock that is projected upon the youth. And, beloved ones, the very serious consideration of the representatives of the Holy Spirit this day is whether or not this generation shall be lost because of the rebellion against love in the misuse of the rhythm in that perverted sound which is invading almost every household where there are young people, and it occurs in youth because of the very energies of the sacred fire. These very energies, then, are those that are desired by the fallen ones.

The invasion of the temple, the invasion of the holy of holies by these unclean spirits through the perversion of sound was the cause of the sinking of Lemuria and Atlantis. I tell you truly, this rhythm is not to be trifled with. It is one thing for the perversion to be in the outer courts of mundane life. But when those who are Keepers of the Flame — upon whose altars we depend for the cleansing of the planet — allow the undisciplined energies of their children to be used in this misuse of the sacred fire, for their failure to control, by the Holy Spirit, their very own children, they therefore allow the desecration of the flame.

I sound the warning, then, that unless some have the courage to be in the world of form that fullness of myself, you will find that for want of the discipline of love and of the sacred fire this civilization will complete the three that have been projected by the fallen ones. You have heard that accidents come in threes; this is because the fallen ones misuse the science of the Trinity. Lemuria, the first. Atlantis, the second. Will this continent, then, and this civilization be the third? Beloved ones, all is not secure until the majority of light is in the victory.

Great strides have been won and the children of the light have to be commended; for without your dynamic decrees, without your attunement with these very bhajans, there would have been far greater cataclysm in the North American continent during this winter cycle. We see, then, inroads of light penetrating the deepest levels of the astral plane. We see that penetration of the mental belt. And yet, as the release of rays of light, unless there is sufficient thrust and momentum by the fiery flame of purity, the resistance to that light, as friction on the highway, causes the penetration to ultimately come to its farthest reach. And thus we need a greater penetration of the Alpha current, of the masculine ray, of souls raised up in the understanding of the carrying of that light. We need mothers who are in the flame of Mother who carry and are the guardian spirits of the children. Blessed ones, the temple must be secure.

Let the teaching, then, concerning the misuse of music be spread abroad. Let the appreciation of the great works of those classic composers who were sent by the Lords of Karma to manifest the inner pattern of the music of the inner spheres be taught to the children, be taught to the adults. Let them be saturated with the inner harmony of the soul and thereby have the discriminating faculty of the Christ mind. Beloved ones, the Lords of Karma anticipated the age when the fallen ones would emerge by the voodoo rhythm from the very pit of the astral plane. And therefore, centuries upon centuries before this hour of crisis upon Terra when mankind would be destined to meet the dweller on the threshold, the Lords of Karma have sent forth the great composers to show the people of light what is the proper mode and rhythm and expression of harmony.

Beloved ones, in golden-age societies — in the etheric culture — those who give forth music are required to have a certain attainment on the path of self-mastery. They are required to be under a guru and to have balanced the energy of love. Those who give forth the music in these cultures and civilizations, which I tell you exist on many planets and systems of worlds, are honored for their level of attain-

Penetration of astral plane

Need penetration of Alpha current

Misuse of music

Voodoo rhythm ... pit

Golden-age societies

Guru — energy balance

ment. And it is absolutely not permitted that those who engage in astral or psychic activities be allowed to put forth the sound, the energy of rhythm, or a voice on behalf of the people. Those who sing and those who play musical instruments become the harmony of an entire planetary body. Upon their chakras and within their temples, the cosmic chords of the Elohim vibrate. And it is understood that sound as a wavelength, as an energy, penetrates the sphere, the habitation, the planet, even if it is not heard by its inhabitants.

Pollution of airways, TV, radio, media

And thus, beloved ones, it is unthinkable that the fallen ones should ever have the freedom to pollute the mainstream of consciousness as upon earth. The airways, the television, the radio, and the entire media of communication have been turned over to those rhythms which come forth from death, from the fallen ones, and from the arch-deceivers.

Jazz

Beloved ones, there is nothing, and I say *nothing whatsoever* that is constructive in *any* form of jazz. And I say this unequivocally. And if you desire to have Shiva in your midst, you will hear the truth straight from that focus of the sacred fire which I AM. And if you would hear the truth and if you would be the truth and if you would be ready for the touch of Shiva and for the initiation, you must understand that those who have come into our meetings challenging the messenger on this point of the law are themselves invaded by the very unclean spirits who are the spirit of this form of music.

I will not let go of this subject because so many of the students of the light have taken it lightly and have not heeded the word of the Mother. And therefore they have not resisted the immense magnetism of these fallen ones who are pulling down, by their spiral of their rhythm, an entire civilization. Beloved ones, we have seen this destruction in various systems of the world. It is not new. It is the same old devil-beat of Mara and the hordes of light.

Destruction of civilization in systems of worlds

Devil-beat of Mara

Blessed and beloved ones, I release the scourge of sacred fire to cleanse the earth of de-

Cleanse earth of demons

mons. Shall I then stand for that infamy that those whose temples have been cleansed again and again by the Elohim will then allow what they consider to be a harmless pastime, a harmless then allowing of that energy to be the background noise in their homes, in their businesses? Beloved ones, it is an encroachment of your free will.

Prayer in schools

They have denied prayer in the schools because it is the encroachment upon the free will of the fallen ones who have denied God in the person of the Father, the Son, and of the Holy Spirit. They have brought to the schools instead sex education from the earliest levels.

Supreme Court

Can you tell me why there is not a cry in the land of the sons and daughters of God standing before the Supreme Court and saying: "You are interfering with my religious freedom to train my children according to the uses of the sacred fire. This is my religion. You are interfering with it. You are interfering with my right as a parent to raise up my children according to the laws of God and human dignity." No, there is not a cry in the land. It is barren of those who have the courage to be unpopular with the world and those who are burdened, then, by pollution, by chemicals, by smoking, by every form of degrading element including that which has become pornography in advertising, in national magazines right on the very pages of those magazines which are considered to be the standbys.

Courage to be unpopular

Pollution by chemicals, smoking... pornography

Cosmic dance

Beloved ones, the horrendous misuse of the body of the Mother must be stopped. I demand it! I AM Shiva, and I stand in the United States of America on the wast side of the City Foursquare, and I perform my cosmic dance, and I dance upon the demons and I say: *Woe* to those who ignore my call! *Woe* to those who will sin against the Holy Ghost by the misuse of love! *Woe* to those who in their rebellion have persisted in the perversion of the sacred fire!

Perversion of sacred fire

I tell you, God has laws. And no matter what the rationalization of the fallen ones, those laws are the same yesterday, today, and forever. Free will, indeed! Free will to destroy oneself. Well I tell you, we will not allow that free will of the fallen ones to destroy the light-bearers. But the light-bearers themselves must shout with a mighty voice, must take the mission seriously and move as one flank, as the coordinates of Shiva, as the Holy Spirit legions of light.

Shiva in Congress

Let there be, then, the action of Shiva in the Congress. I stand in the chambers of the Congress in this moment. I release the energy of the light of Brahma, Vishnu, and Shiva. *Bolts* of blue lightning descend! *Bolts* of white fire descend! *Bolts* of pink lightning descend from the heart of the Great Central Sun! I AM the judgment. I AM the coming of the trial by fire. I AM that trial by fire in the office of the

President in White House

President, in the White House, in the Congress, and in the Supreme Court, and I say *Woe* to the fallen ones who have invaded this temple, *woe!* for the Trinity of Almighty God is come. I say, then, let there be light-bearers who are willing to ensoul this, the judgment, as the Lords of Karma send forth the light and the rebuke of those fallen prophets and

False pastors

false pastors of the people.

Obelisk of Atlantis, Manhattan

Beloved ones, I stand now in Manhattan. I stand in the center of the obelisk brought long ago from Egypt. I stand in the center of that pillar. I radiate energies to the obelisks of Atlantis at that point in London and in Egypt and wherever upon earth this sacred form is manifest, and I send forth a

Electrodes of energy

light of white fire. These electrodes of energy will release on a time cycle certain energies of the Mother — of the Shakti of Brahma, Vishnu, and Shiva and the Mother light within you.

Beloved ones, the coming of this light to those who are not aligned with the light is "outer darkness," is the "weeping and gnashing of teeth." I say, this is the hour when the sons and daughters of God

Twin flames must align

as twin flames must align and hold now, *hold* the circle of fire, that time and space might be preserved yet a little while and the nations of the earth and the people of the earth. For God seeks a greater harvest. And, beloved ones, I tell you the reason for the withholding and the staying action of the judgment of the fallen ones in the presence of this great injustice against Almighty God is because, precisely, the children of the light have not aligned themselves with the light; and therefore, should the judgment come now it would also destroy the people of light.

Therefore, in the great mercy of Almighty God there has been a holding action of cataclysm and of the collapse of the economy. And Saint Germain has told our messenger that the greatest opposition to the light of love in America today is the hatred of America directed right at the level of the economy, and there at the dollar, and there at the gold supply, and there at the balance of the nation and the flow of currency on the national and international markets. Beloved ones, were it not for the presence in embodiment of the messenger and the chelas, I tell you the economy of this nation would have already collapsed. And this is a truth which I bear to you that you might understand how powerful is that light that is held in this dispensation. And I give tribute to the children of the light who have already become aware of the teachings of Saint Germain in South America and in the other nations of the earth, for they, too, have held the flame.

Beloved ones, the first line of attack of the fallen ones is to use mankind's karma against them in this very flow of energy, in the flow of the wheels of commerce, the distribution of food, of energy, electricity, water, and all that is necessary for day-to-day life. As you have seen in periods of blackout or of untoward weather conditions, these services are easily disrupted and with that disruption not many days need pass before chaos, starvation, and mass epidemic. Beloved ones, civilization itself is held upon the tenuous thread of the ability of the individual to sustain the contact with the inner light, for those in embodiment who hold the reins of power in these areas of service do not have the actual at-

Cataclysm

Hatred of America

Economy and gold

Collapse of economy

Attack against flow of energy

Blackouts, weather disruption, starvation

tainment to meet the opposition that is leveled against those strongholds that are the service of the people.

Beloved ones, the second line of attack that is so serious against the light-bearers of every nation is the manipulation of karma, world karma, by the fallen ones in weather conditions and in cataclysm. Some of these fallen ones are in embodiment and some of them have learned to manipulate weather; others are in the astral plane who are misusing that energy that has already been misqualified by mankind. And thus elemental life are the victims of the practice of black magic, sorcery, and witchcraft by those demons who are the imposters of the hierarchy of the Holy Spirit.

Understand, then, that between the attack upon the economy and the balance of forces in nature, this is the line which you must hold, this is where light must be placed, this is where electrodes must be actually inserted by your conscious calls in the etheric, mental, emotional, and physical belts of the earth. [To be concluded in next week's *Pearl of Wisdom.*]

Beloved ones, when you have the mass build-up of pollution, you have many elmentals who are incapacitated and unable, then, to use their body temples as a point of transmutation of mankind's karma. They become so burdened by the physical pollution that therefore they are limited as to how much energy of the karma itself they may transmute, and thus you see the stepping up of cataclysm. Wherever there is cataclysm you must understand that it is because nature, the Holy Spirit, demands a balance of light and darkness. And because it has not been transmuted in the threefold flame of the sons and daughters of God or by the light-bearers because they have not been sufficient in number or dedicated enough to call forth the light, then it spills over into the economy and into the elemental kingdom.

You will watch, then, how crisis is produced month after month in these levels, and you will see

Manipulation of world karma

Black magic, sorcery, demons

Build up of pollution

Limit of karma transmuted by elementals

Balance of light/darkness

the signs of the times when you feel the burden upon the economy or elemental life that you must come together in your groups for the multiplication of dynamic decrees. This is during those certain peak periods when the energy becomes most intense.

I speak then on the plot of the fallen ones to take out from the control of this nation the nexus of Panama Canal   light that is at the Panama Canal. Beloved ones, the Panama Canal is not a mere physical canal. It is the nexus of the flow of energy between North and South America, the very nexus of the Christ consciousness; it is the flow of water, and it is the place consecrated for the distribution of that energy. Just as the figure eight within your temple is the flow of light, so there is a flow of light between northern and southern hemispheres, and this is necessary that the polarity of Alpha and Omega at the poles may be kept. And thus you see, beloved ones, it has naught to do with goodwill or with the signs of the times or the elimination of so-called imperialism; it has naught to do with karma or justice or injustice Flow of energy North   surrounding Panama, her history; but it has solely to and South America   do with the fact that the fallen ones desire to see those with less light, less attainment, less stable governments be in control and thereby the light itself at inner levels is betrayed and it is left unprotected.

America invaded   America may have been invaded, her armed
Morale   forces compromised, there may be a weakening of the morale of the people but I tell you still, of all the nations of the earth, she holds the greatest promise for the incorporation of light within the planetary body. And, beloved ones, there is not another nation America's capacity to   which has the capacity to defend freedom upon the defend freedom   earth outside of this nation. And therefore you will see the total loss of freedom upon Terra, as there has been the total loss of freedom and light upon Mars through the take-over of the astral hordes, should the people of this nation not carry the torch of love, of wisdom, and of power in this age.

Beloved ones, it is interesting to note some-

South Africa, Rhodesia,
carry great light

No approval apartheid
policies

thing which you may be very surprised to learn and that is that the nations of South Africa and of Rhodesia themselves have carried a great light in the African continent. Of course, we have no approval of the apartheid policies but always the understanding of levels of karma, levels of attainment with the firm conviction of absolute opportunity for training, for education — both spiritual and material — for every citizen, everyone who has come forth from the land.

Nevertheless, beloved ones, despite this disparaging situation caused by the division and the plots of the fallen ones, these nations themselves still have the opportunity to hold a great light. And therefore we ask the student body to pray for the resolving of conflict, the resolving of inequities, the resolving of the abuse of those who are the sons and daughters of Afra within those nations. We are calling to you to give your decrees for the preservation of the light; for you see, beloved ones, the fallen ones have fomented a tremendous strife and a condemnation of the people of these nations when it is the few fallen ones in government who pursue a policy that is not according to the Lords of Karma.

Intent of fallen ones in
Soviet Union

Bloodbath beyond
compare

Communist Revolution
Capitalist conspirators

Beyond this we must look, then, to the intent of the fallen ones who are in positions of power in the Soviet Union to take control of the Indian Ocean, the ports, the waterways, the minerals, the resources, the tremendous wealth of South Africa, and to use the excuse of racial division to cause a bloodbath that would be beyond compare in the history of Africa should it come to pass. And if it come to pass, I tell you it will be the detriment of the cause of world freedom and to the increase of the amalgamation of power in the hands of the fallen ones — the Communist Revolution and the capitalist conspirators that back them.

Yes, beloved ones, I am on the line of the Holy Spirit and I see clearly every demon and discarnate who has invaded the temples of light. I see how there has been the contriving of the manipulation of peoples, I see the manipulation in the Middle East as the Arabs and the Jews are pitted against one another in an age-old strife that began long ago beyond this planetary body. And as they have come to earth, they have imported with them that hatred for one of the other — of their descendants and those who have come forth in the beginning from the same seed and from the same flame of the Mother.

Beloved ones, this strife augmented by so many divisions and so many individuals seeking power within the Middle East has been long considered the trump card of the fallen ones. If all else fails, they still intend to explode that condition in the Middle East. And therefore I send forth the call of light that you might receive now the energy of Shiva within you to be the ones who also give the cry *Shiva!* into the cause and core of this manipulation. Beloved ones, the entire Middle East is a setup. It is a setup of the fallen ones and the conspiracy of the fallen ones.

Middle East — trump card of fallen ones — a set up

Precious hearts of light, America is the Promised land. It is the place prepared for the sons and daughters of God. Who are, then, the usurpers who would attempt to manipulate real estate, land, wealth, oil, and all of the resources? Those among both Arabs and Jews and those who are the imposters of both moving among them, for the fallen ones have also embodied among the Arabs and the Jews to take advantage of that karma that has existed between them. You see, beloved ones, there is nothing simple and there are no simple solutions. For when you have the added x factor of the fallen ones, there is not the ability to work line upon line with situations of karma and dharma but always the manipulation and always the temptation of the children of God to stray, then, from the light and to desire the things of this world.

Manipulation of real estate, oil, wealth, resources

It is human greed and selfishness, it is the selfish misuse of the light of the Holy Spirit that has brought down upon the children of God and the children of Israel century after century these wars manipulated by the fallen ones to the destruction of

Human greed, selfishness — destruction of children of God

the children of light. This is my message as I stump across America and the nations of the earth with the Mother. For I AM Shiva, and I AM the original stumper, and I go forth with my dance upon the demons even as the Mother becomes the mouth-piece of my flame. We are determined to have our

Victory in this age victory in this age. And I tell you, the legions of Shiva and of Kali and of Durga are the fierce ones, and none can stand our gaze except those who have the same unflinching zeal and devotion to the truth.

We are not concerned with those who love the path of compromise; they are neither hot nor cold, they are spewed out of the mouth of God and out of our presence. We march forward with those who have the zeal of the sacred fire, and we do not count the numbers of the people — we do not number the amount of those who have signed up for this or that.

Factor of light We number the factor of light, the cosmic cross of white fire, and the cube in the heart. And, beloved ones, I may tell you that when the measure of light is measured by weight and the measure of darkness is measured by weight, then you will see how the little

Light-bearers compose less than 1% world population band of light-bearers composing far less than one percent of earth's population will be the majority with God.

Have you considered that the pressing on of this opportunity to now enlist many new light-bearers in the teachings of the ascended masters has come forth from our deliberations? For we see

Calculate how much light to hold the balance and we calculate precisely how much light by how much karma, by how much attainment is neces-sary; and you would be amazed to realize how few more, comparatively speaking, are required to actually hold the balance for the turning of light in this age. Beloved ones, it will not take millions but thousands — a certain thousands of souls that I am calling forth, certain souls who are numbered. In fact, my very flame rests just above their head so that when they hear the voice and the call of the Mother, that flame will descend into their hearts and they will know her face and know that message and know that Word and begin to give those daily calls.

Lord Christ

Hard sell

Relentless light of Shiva
will wear away
hardness of heart

Sacred fire dissolving
props of human ego

Wedding garment

Frequency of energy

Beloved ones, I enlist you in stumping. I send you forth two by two as the Lord Christ sent forth the other seventy two by two into the cities. I tell you, become mobile. Go out into the highways and byways and *compel* them to come in! Beloved ones, there is hard sell in advertising for liquor, for cigarettes, and for the promotion of every form of darkness. Let there be the hard sell, the compelling sell of the threefold flame of the avatars! Let that light be invincible and victorious! Let it be unanimous! Let it be relentless!

O beloved ones, see how the relentless drippings of the water wears away the granite. See how the relentless light of Shiva will wear away even the hardness of men's hearts, even the most recalcitrant, even the most rebellious ones. Ah, Shiva will have you yet for that sacred fire! You who are born of God, you will not remain long outside. For I will begin to ignite that flame, and you will begin to feel that heat, and with the heat the melting of the wax of illusion until the pinions of your pride will fall to the ground and all of the feathers with which you have feathered your nest and your pride and all of that substance which is unreal. Beloved ones, by the intense fervor of the sacred fire there is the literal dissolving of all of the props of the human ego until ultimately, through the test of Shiva, the individual must stand naked in the sacred fire. And those who are clothed are those who have on the wedding garment.

I will not further burden you with my energy nor tire you, but I will stand before you to give you that touch of Shiva — to extend to your chakras a certain frequency and a certain energy which will then immediately be transmitted to your twin flame. This I give to you. And I will come again on another occasion for the same dispensation, but it will not be given at any time except it be given in person through the dictation that I am bringing forth. This is necessary, beloved ones, because of the nature of the light and energy of the Holy Spirit. For the same reason, Lord Christ gave the command to teach in all nations and to baptize them in the name of the Father, the Son, and of the Holy Ghost. This baptism is performed, then, by our messenger by that physical contact, and so it is. There be some initiations that can be passed etherically, mentally, or at the level of the desire body. But in the Holy Spirit light, it is the physical contact; and thus we have sent forth our messengers through the ages.

Salute you in love

I salute you in love. I commend you for the tremendous effort of light. I commend the staff, the Keepers of the Flame, and every light-bearer upon earth who has upheld the staff — the rod of energy. And you who have failed to do so by your discord, I say, *Shame* upon you in this hour! How dare you stand in the service of God or our messenger and release those discordant energies which are the betrayal of the very flame! And you yourselves who have not been a part of this activity yet who call yourselves devotees of the flame, you who have allowed discord and contempt and hatred and disdain into your lives by the justification of spiritual pride, I say, *Shame* upon you! You have not escaped my eye, for the eye of Shiva is upon the elect of God.

The eye of Shiva upon elect of God
Come up to the standard
Forsake lesser activities, come into worship of light
The hour is very late

And those who are of the elect, then, let them come up to standard! Let them be willing to be disciplined! Let them forsake those lesser activities and come *now* into our training, into our university, into our workshop of light! For the acceleration of light is on, and the hour is very late.

I AM *Shiva!* of the flame.

Lady Master Venus

April 1978

Hail, O light within the cloven tongues of fire that God in his desiring has sent forth to conquer a cosmos and to ensoul it with love — only the love of twin flames.

I stand in your midst rejoicing to be received in the chalice of the pink rose of the love of Keepers of the Flame and devotees of the light in this city, New York. Here in this island, once an island of light in days of Atlantis, I center the flame of Mother and the diamond light of my heart for a purpose. And I have come to tell you of the fall of Babylon. Babylon that great city, how art thou fallen? And in the prophecy given by the Lord Christ unto John that is recorded in the Book of Revelation is come to pass in this age as the cities of the Earth have entered into the spirals of degeneration which caused the prophet of old to cry out, 'Babylon, Babylon, how art thou fallen?"

Understand, then, that when there is the corruption of the Matter plane by the misuse of the sacred fire, the cycles of the feminine ray descend to dissolve — by the action of Lord Shiva and the Holy Spirit — that which has been the misuse of the

Mother principle of life. And therefore the fall that is registering even now in the cities of the Earth is the descending spiral, that negative energy that is for the dissolution of miscreation in order that at the base of the Pyramid of Life souls of light may once again call forth the caduceus light of Alpha and

Etheric blueprint Omega and resurrect the etheric blueprint of the City Foursquare that is intended to be the foundation of life on Earth beginning with the spiritual centers, the great cities of the Earth. And so in this city of New York — key city of the release of light, key city where the corruption and abuse has resulted in now the descent of that negative spiral — I AM come.

Blessed ones, the dispensation for my coming to Earth in this decade was made possible from the

Cosmic Council Cosmic Council and the Lords of Karma because there was upon Earth a group of devotees ensoul-

Messenger ing the Mother light and the messenger devoted to that light, and thus the coordinates necessary for our coming were in physical manifestation upon Earth. Without these devotees, without this messenger and those who are following the Ancient of Days, throughout the Earth, it could not have been accorded that I should come as I have told you a number of years ago to keep the flame of love and of the Mother and of light even as my beloved twin flame, Sanat Kumara, did keep the flame for Earth.

And so I am tarrying these years, and likewise my coming to this city — again the dispensation of light — is made possible only by the calls of light by those who inhabit this island and the surrounding areas. Understand, then, that the greatest gratitude of the ascended masters and of the souls of all

Christ Self mankind and of the Christ Self of each one is given unto you, each and every one, who could find in your life the moments to give adoration to God, to set aside this weekend, to gather here. For *you* are

Living chalice the living chalice, and there is no other chalice whereby we may appear.

Beloved ones, the sending of souls of light to found the teaching center in this city has been the

Alchemy — in
prophecy, option of
souls

Averting cataclysm

Exposure of deception

Billions of elementals

Evolutionary platform
threshing floor for the
judgment

Dissolution of
miscreation in cities

Energy stripped from
fallen ones

Fall of stars

Purging of a planet and
a people

Path of initiation
Electrodes of light

means of an alchemy in prophecy that is always the
option of souls in embodiment who by free will may
hear the prophecy of the Lord God and understand
themselves to be the instrument of averting cataclysm and of bringing to pass the overriding spirals
of light that through the alchemy of the Holy Spirit
can dissolve, defeat, and bring about the victory.

And so we are witnessing in this city simultaneously with the exposure of deception, simultaneously with the activities of the fallen ones
aggressively manifesting themselves against the
light, an action of the new birth, the bubbling of the
resurrection flame that is seen coming from deep
within the heart of the Earth from twin flames who
ensoul the sun of even pressure in the heart of the
Earth — from Virgo and Pelleur, Aries and Thor,
Neptune and Luara, Oromasis and Diana — key
hierarchs of light who govern the release of the
Trinity and of the Mother through billions of elementals who are serving to preserve this city and
America and the nations of the Earth as an
evolutionary platform for the souls of light and as
the threshing floor for the judgment of the fallen
ones.

And therefore, two distinct activities are seen
simultaneously upon the Earth. Even as in the
Matter plane and in the dissolution of miscreation
within the cities, so within the hearts of the inhabitants of the Earth there is at once the degeneration
spiral whereby, through the initiation of Lord Shiva,
there is being stripped from the laggards and the
fallen ones all energy they have misused. This, then,
is 'the fall' — the fall of those stars who once
occupied positions of great light. And therefore the
stars of the heavens, those who have exalted
themselves, have been cast down to the Earth.

Parallel to this activity, so necessary for the
purging of a planet and a people by the judgment of
love, there exists the path of initiation. And each of
those who is spiraling through that path, each one
becomes an electrode for the raising up of the true
Mother light which is indeed a spiral of the feminine

principle and the negative polarity of the Spirit positive energy. But that negative polarity is not abuse or misuse, it is simply the T'ai chi and the energy in balance of the creation of worlds.

Fine line between truth and error

And so, beloved ones, the reason that there is such a fine line between truth and error in this octave is that both are occupying that Matter spiral, that energy of the Mother; and the negative energy which constitutes a misuse of the Mother polarity is but a shade apart from the true Mater-realization whereby you ensoul the pristine purity of the Mother of the universe, Omega, and whereby you raise up the Mother flame. And until you know the true vibration of the Mother light, beloved ones, it is easy

Glamour of the psychic, false teaching

to think that the glamour of the psychic and the false teaching of the fallen ones and even the energies which they transmit are the real light.

Path of light, path of darkness

Thus we have a path of light, a path of darkness. And so the fallen ones would like to take their misuse of the Mother flame and say, this is the polarity of God; and they have created a philosophy

False polarity philosophy

whereby they have declared that this negative energy is actually in polarity with the light of Spirit, the masculine ray. Beloved ones, good and evil are never in polarity, the energy veil has no magnet of itself to be a part of Spirit. And therefore the eternal

Father-Mother God in you

polarity of the divine lovers, of the Father-Mother God within you, has naught to do with the imitations of the fallen ones.

Imposters of twin flames

You have heard me speak of the imposters of twin flames. Well let me speak today of the imposter of your own path and your own role, always just a shade removed from the original matrix. Therefore understand that it is by purity's light, as the fiery core of each and every chakra, that you will walk as that two-edged sword and be clean of the attraction of any of the particles of darkness that have been scattered in the Earth.

Let purity abound in the wisdom of the mind to His glory. Let purity of vision be upon the altar as each one does kneel and, facing the east, bow to the sun of light. Let purity be reflected in every word, and let the motive and desire of the heart and the great expansive desire body be only to do those things which are pleasing unto the Lord God. Let the desiring of every heart be to see and know him as he is and not to control or impress or manipulate or deceive others or be the instrument of the lie that would mock and challenge the office of the great gurus of light. Beloved ones, let truth within the soul be the liberating force whereby your soul may rise upon the resurrection fire of the fountain of light. Rise then, O soul, rise to meet the soul of the beloved twin flame, and let not the imposters deter you from your path.

Truth within soul the liberating force

Beloved ones, I am here now for the action of the stripping of the soul within your seat-of-the-soul chakra. I am here to strip that soul of the glamour, the effluvia, of the false personality cult — the glamour of this world. I am here to translate to you an action of sacred fire as a cleansing water, as a magnetic energy whereby that which is not of the light is demagnetized from you, and your soul, then, may be in that perfect polarity to the soul of your twin flame whether ascended or unascended. I am here, then, for a momentous arcing of light; for this dedication is unto the fulfillment of the law of the cycles within this city.

Strip soul of glamour

Demagnetizing you

Arcing light

Precious ones, the bringing together of souls of light in New York is truly a dispensation that is known in our octave as the staying action of the Lord God. The staying of the hand of God does manifest in each and every age when souls of light proportionate to the darkness carry an equivalency of light and even greater light and thereby may within their very temple, by purity and only purity, focus a counterweight and therefore stay the action of cataclysm and of karmic judgment.

Counterweight
Staying action of cataclysm

Saint Germain stands with me upon this platform. He has come to be the electrode of freedom and to hold the balance in this city for a time and times and a half a time and a half again of those cycles ordained by the Goddess of Liberty and the Lords of Karma who keep the temple above

Time and half a time
Cycles ordained

this city — the Temple of the Sun. Saint Germain then plants that focus of freedom within the souls of light-bearers for the arcing of the energy of freedom and of love, and that love fire is now creating an open door whereby the souls of light caught in the astral nets of the wicked, caught then in the illusion of a polarity of evil and good, of darkness misqualified with light — may be cut free by beloved Astrea, by Archangel Michael and the hosts of the Lord.

Astral nets

This dispensation of the staying action of the fall of Babylon within New York comes, then, by decree. And that decree has begun with your decree — your decree each day to be diligent, fastidious in the call that compels the answer, your decree to live your life as a living sacrifice not in sorrow but in joy, the joy of life becoming life within you. Whether you have come to this decision a moment ago or a decade ago or somewhere between beloved hearts, God has heard your commitment and by that commitment he will go forth to save the cities and the nations one by one.

Staying action of fall of Babylon by decree

Commitment

Now, beloved hearts, understand that the holding of the flame against such odds of the amalgamation of power and the manipulation of the all-seeing eye of God and its energies which has occurred within this city can only be sustained by wholeness, and that wholeness is based upon Alpha and Omega in union within each one — upon Alpha and Omega focusing the intensity of the light in you and your twin flame. And so the urgency of the hour that our messenger might be on the way as a pilgrim of light bringing the message of the love of twin flames, anchoring our initiations; for only by that certain arc of light and the holding to that arc within your being can Saint Germain perform that perfect work of this age.

Wholeness based on energy of Alpha and Omega

Now it is the desire of the Knight Commander that I share with you the intent of the fallen ones who have usurped the love of twin flames through the ages. Their destruction of the Babylons of this world has been through the intent to pervert the founda-

Usurped love of twin flames

Pervert flow of energy
through economy

tion of life which is always in the flow of energy in all planes of being that rests squarely upon the economic systems of the nations and upon these, resting the government of the nations. Where there is not the flow of the abundant life, where there is not the sound economy, there is the fundamental misuse of the Mother flame. For the Mother flame is the nourishing of the children of God throughout the Matter cosmos, and the energy which you require in your four lower bodies ultimately comes to rest upon your ability to survive in an economic world.

Ability to survive in an
economic world

Beloved ones, the fallen ones see this clearly whereas the children of the light — already free from the desire of the things of this world or of the love of money that is the root of all evil — are not so concerned, then, with that which is happening at the very base level of the manipulation of light through the *mani-pollution* of the economy of this nation which has its foundation here within this city — on Wall Street, in the banking houses, as well as in the government of the city and the mismanagement of the light supply of the people.

Pollution of the
economy

Beloved ones, understand then that the archdeceivers of mankind have always used the flow of supply — even the flow of light and energy at all levels through the chakras — to destroy and pervert the souls of the people; for to destroy the platform of evolution is to destroy the body temple. To destroy the opportunity for you to balance your karma by the law of supply and demand based upon the golden rule is to clip your wings, is to cut off the flow of energy and the moving stream of consciousness, to deprive you of the lawful cycles where by your evolution, your ascent into the resurrection flame, is guaranteed through the path of initiation.

Archdeceivers
destruction of flow of
light

Clip wings — cut off
flow of energy

Archangel Uriel

May 1974

Intensify spirals of light
Intensify spirals of
darkness
Judgment is come to
the planet

Court of Sacred Fire

14 months to bend the
knee

Rebellion

Angels waiting to
separate fallen ones
from those who
chose path of light

Ho! I AM come in the fullness of the flame of the Prince of Peace! I AM Uriel Archangel! I AM Uriel of the Light! And I come to intensify the spirals of light! And I come to intensify the spirals of darkness, for judgment is come upon this planet and this people this day.

I come directly from the Court of the Sacred Fire on the God Star Sirius, where the judgment of the Four and Twenty Elders is meted out. I come then with a proclamation for the fallen ones.

Fourteen months ago you were given opportunity to bend the knee, to confess the Christ — the Christ as the light of every man, the Christ as mediator. In fourteen months some of you have responded. Some of you have come into alignment as you have felt the white heat of judgment drawing high. But others have stood with the forces of rebellion and have resisted the mercy of opportunity.

To you I say, this day the door of opportunity is closed. And my angels and legions of Sanat Kumara and of the Son of God are waiting even now at the very door to separate the fallen ones from

those who have chosen the path of light. And they
shall be bound and separated and cast into outer
Weeping, gnashing of teeth — darkness where there shall be weeping and gnashing of teeth.

The notable day of the Lord's victory is at hand.
The light is oncoming and judgment is rendered.
This day the judgment of Antichrist is proclaimed.
Specifically, all those who have aligned their con-
sciousness against the Son of God receive the
judgment of the Most High God.

I come then before the Court of the Sacred Fire
Plead case of holy innocents — to plead the case of the holy innocents, those
innocent ones who have volunteered to come to
Life snuffed out by abortionists — earth and whose life has been snuffed out by the
hand of the abortionist. I plead on behalf of those
souls who cry out in their mothers' wombs and who
are at the hands and at the mercy of the dark ones,
Scientists of Atlantis — scientists of Atlantis and those whom they have
perverted.

And I say: In the name of God this day, all who
Judgment before God those who have served to legalize abortion — have promoted, all who have served to legalize
abortion, all who have declared abortion as a means
of murdering the Christ stand as judged before
Almighty God. And every state and every nation
which has consented to this crime against the
Christ must also be judged with Antichrist. For to
murder the holy ones is to murder God as flaming
potential — is to crucify him anew. Better for these
that a millstone were hung about their necks, that
they were cast to the bottom of the sea, than to
receive this judgment. I say then, come out from
among them and be a separate people; for judgment is nigh and the descent of that judgment will
be swift and sudden.

10,001 — descend to earth, some aborted — You have heard of the ten thousand and one
who would descend to earth. Now I declare to you
the abomination of desolation standing in the holy
place where it ought not! Some of these little ones
who came forth with valor and courage have
already been aborted at the hands of these scien-
Herod's sword — tists! Those who hold the sword of Herod to kill the
newborn child have done their work, and thus the

Finding parents for the
10,001

They will not be denied

Woe to all who have
aborted cycles

Every jot and tittle of the
law will be fulfilled

Opportunity denied

Better to be totally
aligned with light

America repent — time
is short

Wrath of fire of Holy
Ghost will divide light
from darkness

earth is judged this day. I tell you before the Court of
the Sacred Fire, their souls are undaunted. And
these holy ones, when we can find parents who are
true and honorable in the sight of God, will come
forth again. And the manifestation of the ten
thousand and one will not be denied, will not be held
back!

I say to all: Woe to you who have prevented the
cycles of manifestation! Woe to you who have
aborted the Christ consciousness! I say this day: By
the hand of the Great Divine Director, there is
released the spiral of the abortion of the fulfillment
of the divine plan within you. You shall go back to
that place of darkness, and you shall know that
which you have inflicted upon life until every jot and
tittle of the law is fulfilled. One day you will stand
before the Lords of Karma and plead for life, for
opportunity, for incarnation; and it will be denied.
And not until the last farthing is paid will opportunity
be granted again to you for incarnation.

Let those who have chosen the Christ and to
sponsor the Christ align their energies with the
Christ consciousness in every facet of being. For
when the judgment of Antichrist and those who are
a part of this vicious misrepresentation of the law is
meted out, I tell you it would be better that you
would be aligned with light totally than to preserve
one erg, one facet of consciousness of the carnal
mind, lest you be scorched by those sacred fires
that shall surely come upon those who have done
this wicked thing in this age.

O America, repent! Repent in this hour, for the
time is short and the Lord God of Hosts Himself is
come down to you with great wrath! And the wrath is
the kindling fire of the Holy Ghost and the action of
the law. And it shall divide the way of light from
darkness. Therefore, O people of light, come apart
and declare the truth! For God in you is yet able to
raise up a community of light-bearers to preserve
the light and the law for a golden age.

I have spoken out of the mouth of God for and
on behalf of the Four and Twenty Elders. And you

will hear the fullness of their message and of this judgment at the Convocation of the New Birth. My sword i ، thrust into the ground, and it transmits the rod of fire from the altar of the Most High God! And the atoms of the earth do quiver and tremble as the electrode of Almighty God brings into alignment light with light, darkness with darkness, that it might be no more, that death might be swallowed up in victory.

My legions come forth; and they gather north, south, east, and west the souls of the holy innocents who have been sacrificed at the hands of the modern Herods. The souls are garnered into the storehouse of the Lord; and they shall be kept there for a time, times, and a half a time until the opportunity is extended to mankind once again to bring forth those whom they have murdered. They know not that they have pronounced already the death of their own souls by this act and that they could not in all eternity destroy life, for life is God. And the law is the law. And that law is pronounced this day as judgment. So be it.

Atoms of earth quiver

Electrode of Almighty God brings into alignment light with light

Modern Herods

Opportunity to bring forth those they have murdered

Pronouncing death of very own souls

The law is judgment

Mother Liberty

1976

Gaps in evolutionary chain

Absence of lifestreams

I am a mother of the Mother flame in cosmic dimensions and I am very conscious of the gaps in the evolutionary chain of hierarchy now occurring on Terra. I am concerned with coming decades and the absence of those lifestreams who have been denied opportunity to live, to move, to breathe, to overcome, to attain God-mastery on Terra.

Denial of entrance of avatars — warning to mankind

Cataclysm

Fodder for manipulators

Make own bed, lie in it — karma

What will you do in twenty-five years when the scientists and the great avatars and those who espouse mankind's freedom, those who are not returning to liberate the masses, are not there because you have denied them life? What will you do when the ages turn, when there are wars and rumors of wars and pestilence and plague and cataclysm taking the life of many, when the dearth of population comes and there is not the replacement for those souls whose karma will take them from the screen of life? What will you do, O mankind who have made yourselves prey — fodder — for the manipulators? You have believed the lie; and as it is written, your condemnation is just, because you will have made your own karma. As you say, you make your own bed and you lie in it.

This is the story of karma; karma is the exercise of free will. I ask you now, have you exercised free will or have you been manipulated? You do not exercise free will until you know both sides of the story. Did you know this side of the story before I spoke to you? Did you know that there are thousands of Christed ones awaiting incarnation? You have been told of their courage. You have heard that they come, they are aborted, and they volunteer again, knowing that they may pass through the trauma of dying in their mother's wombs. Yet they volunteer again because they are determined to set life free!

They are far more determined than many of mankind embodied to liberate the masses; for they see above and beyond the manipulation of the death cult; and therefore they see your souls crying out, pleading with the Lords of Karma for help, for intercession. They behold the prayers of children; they behold the praying of babies in their mothers' wombs praying for life, praying they will come to maturation to be born in Mater — souls waiting to incarnate who are mature, advanced lifestreams not only from Terra but from other planetary bodies and even volunteers from other systems of worlds.

They have knocked on the doors of the Lords of Karma in our chambers in the Royal Teton Retreat. They have pleaded for opportunity. We have shown them what they will be up against and yet they have said: "We will go; we will try! We will work with mothers and fathers; we will find our place. We will find room in the inn on Terra." And so they come and they continue to come.

Now see what the question of abortion brings as karma to the feet of a nation! See what war brings as karma to the feet of a nation! Understand that those who kill with the sword must be killed by the sword. Whether the sword is on the battlefield or in the surgeon's hand, the taking of life bears the consequence. And these consequences place a heavy karma on the people of America whose

Margin notes

Thousands of Christed ones awaiting embodiment

Volunteers aborted again

Death cult of masses

Soul volunteers from other worlds waiting to incarnate

Abortion and karma to the nation

Kill by sword — be killed by sword

Christ consciousness   destiny it is to bring forth the Christ consciousness
    of the heart   not only in the little children, but through the sacred
fires of the heart....

El Morya

1974

Certainty of
reincarnation

"Do you know the hour of your coming and your going, of your aborning in the womb of time and your moving again through space to other shores? Are you certain that you will reincarnate in another embodiment? Are you not concerned with the problem of abortion? Are you not concerned that if you do not attain on the Path [of soul evolution] in this life, that you may very well be aborted again and again and again as the race spirals into greater and greater selfishness and the denial of the birth of the Divine Manchild? And where will you go to balance your karma? Where will you go to fulfill your inner blueprint?"[1]

Race spirals into
selfishness
Denial of birth
Balance karma

Embryonic life is
tabernacle
Sons of Belial kill

Crucify Jesus
Penalty of crucifying
Christ

From the moment of conception, embryonic life is the tabernacle of the Lord. When the sons of Belial sought to kill the Christ, they could not; for the eternal Christ is the light that lighteth every man that cometh into the world. When they crucified Jesus instead, they incurred the penalty of crucifying the Christ. For to destroy the temple is to effectively destroy the manifestation of the Christ in time and space....

Life no longer sacred

Eternal values dwindle
— dying embers

Sophistication,
  manipulation
World in ashes

Cannibalism

Massacred

Subhuman evolution
Subanimal

I say to every responsible citizen of every nation upon earth: How can the kingdom of God come into manifestation if you will deny these little ones, if you will abort the cycles of life? Where life is no longer sacred, where selfishness and hardness of heart and sensuality take precedence over the joy of giving birth to the everlasting Christos, there the eternal values dwindle as dying embers; and soon they are no more.

Life must cherish life as the entire cosmos moves with the flow of the Holy Spirit, with the first breath of the newborn child — where all of creation is a rhapsody of praise to the living God and life is the eternal fount whence spring our hope, our faith, our love, and our joy. When those who have received the gift of life from the Holy Spirit use that gift to destroy life, they ultimately destroy themselves.

O humanity, take care that in your sophistication and in your manipulation of life, you do not find the world in ashes beneath your feet. When men begin to destroy their offspring, they reenter the age of cannibalism. Indeed, it is a dark hour for the human race when the people's senses are dulled to the cries of the unborn, the helpless, the unwanted, massacred in their mother's wombs. This is the beginning of the end when mankind enter new lows of self-degradation and the angels look down upon an evolution not subhuman but subanimal; for even the creatures of the forest bring forth their young with reverence for life and endearment.

Portia

January 1978

Abortion of life
Adjust cycles

Adjust cycles

Reallocation of energy

Imbalance in karmic
pattern

Difficulty in resolving
world problems

Ours is to consider the abortion of life and to determine how to adjust the cycles of karma that these souls, these Christs from out the Great Central Sun for whom you have called for so long and who have been sent to you, might reenter the birth canal and be born to serve their cosmic purpose. Beloved ones, to adjust and adjust again the cycles for the appearance of light-bearers is one of the greatest challenges to the Lords of Karma. Greater than any other is the reallocation of the allotment of energy for the millions of souls who are aborted annually.

Such an imbalance in the karmic pattern and the mandala of the earth is at stake in this hour that we can scarcely address ourselves to world conditions or render a report without prefacing our report by stating that this condition is that which makes difficult the resolving of all other conditions upon the planetary body.

Gautama Buddha

May 1974

Deaf ear to cries

And if these who have turned a deaf ear to the cries of the little ones, if these who have become numb and hardened their hearts against souls aborning should hold their peace, should be silent before the edict of God, then I say the very stones will cry out; and the mountains and the hills will rumble, and the adjustment then will come as the violent thrust of the earth, the earth's upheaval to once again rectify the flow of life.

Very stones cry out
Mountains rumble —
  upheaval

If, then, mankind reject that life which is God, they will find that they themselves will be rejected of God. And the Lord God himself through the elemental kingdom and the mighty Elohim will stay the hand of those who break this commandment. And thus, the earth will be shaken, balance will be forthcoming, and a new age and a new cycle will be begun. For I tell you the Lord God will not remain silent before the infamy of mankind, and the desecration of the holy innocents.

Earth shaken
Balance forthcoming
New cycle

... I initiate this day the spiral from my heart that bears the energies of the Elohim, of the very Center of Cosmos, that goes forth to roll back, to reverse the tide and to challenge all doctrine of

Center of Cosmos

Annihilated by own
spirals

Come to restore
balance

Annihilate platform of
evolution

Thou shalt not kill

abortion, of the taking of life, of the life that is God. And I say it shall be no more, for the energy has gone forth. And if mankind do not respond to the edict of the Lords of Karma and of the Lord of the World, they will find themselves annihilated by the spirals which they have initiated against the life of God in these little ones.

I come to restore balance before it is too late. I come to say, in the name of the Cosmic Virgin, receive ye sons and daughters of God, receive ye those who come from on High bearing the flames of Alpha and Omega. O Earth, O mankind, if you persist in this way of darkness you will annihilate your very being and the very platform of your evolution. Therefore, into the ethers, into the mental plane, into the emotional body, into each physical cell and atom I place the law of God. I write it now in the inward parts: thou shalt not kill.

Archangel Zadkiel

February 1977

I speak, then, of the widespread practice of abortion, the aborting of life as fathers and mothers have turned a deaf ear to the cries of the unborn child. This, then, is the returning karma. It is exactly that coldness and that hardness of heart which you have put forth against these souls of light and these children of God, even where there has been the collaboration of parents and doctors who have determined that incoming children with defects ought not to have the opportunity for life. And therefore, they are left without care, even in the hospitals, that they might die because they ought not to have the right to live.

It is a very sad day in the land, for America has led the world in this infamy and in accepting the lie of the fallen ones in the control of population. I tell you, precious hearts, America, then, must bear the burden of this karma, and this type of weather that is upon the people is only the beginning of the returning of that karma, because the people have not heeded the Word of the archangels or of the true prophets in the land.

Spirit of prophecy
Warning unto the
  people
Be obedient to God

Let it go forth, then, that Word which I send this day, that people of every faith and every understanding may at least have contact with that Word and with that message. For the spirit of prophecy is the spirit of warning, and it is the warning unto the people that they ought to be obedient to God if they expect to be blessed and protected by God in this land which the Lord thy God hath given thee.

Jesus

December 1978

Great souls can come to you

Beloved ones, great souls can come to earth to you and to many wonderful families of light in all religions in this year. But the drive toward abortion,

Drive to take life before it's protected

the drive for the taking of the life of the Messiah before it is protected by the fullness of consciousness [descended] is on the increase and therefore must be exposed by enlightenment, by love and by a God determination that invokes the judgment, that confirms the judgment, and that is absolutely determined that the will of God shall prevail in this issue.

Condition of great concern to Mother Mary

Beloved ones, there is not a condition of earth that is of greater concern to Mother Mary in this hour than the protection of children awaiting birth, and the protection of those in embodiment who are sent upon a regal and rightful mission for the Lord.

Disturbance in balance in the planet

...There is a disturbance in the balance of the planet. And the concern of the Mother is that the Great White Brotherhood will no longer be able to stay the hand of the descent of karma on abortion, propounded and extended throughout the earth

Nation America will reap descent of karma

from this nation of America. The time has come, then, when the earth will reap that karma which they

Murder of Holy
Innocents

have brought upon themselves by the murder of the
holy innocents . . .

Many lost sheep

Beloved ones, we cannot speak of Elysian
fields and other glories and other realities while
there is one lost sheep. Today there are many, many
lost sheep who have strayed from the flock, not by
their own doing but because they have been
deterred by those who have wilfully prevented their
birth in life.

Souls of light blocked
entrance

So great is the upset in the balance of the
United States today of those lifestreams who have
been sent for the victory that it is the major subject
of discussion before the Lords of Karma at the
conclusion of this year as to how we will find entrée
for these souls of light and how we will then allow
them to accelerate and to take their place which has
been blocked now for many years even unto a
decade. And so the setting back of evolution by
those days and hours and years; that becomes the
great dilemma.

Setting back of
evolution great
dilemma of Lords of
Karma

Abortion — the issue
upon which all other
issues hang

Beloved ones, let, therefore, the sons and
daughters of God take this issue abortion as the one
in which they determine to be God victorious, for
upon it all other issues hang.

And, beloved children of God, you who are
pursuing the fullness of your own Christ Self
understand, then, that those leaders who will not
take their stand for God and for life must also be
accounted for — those to the right and those to the
left of the law of being.

The tares and the wheat

And so you see, the very issue itself is a dividing
of the way of the tares and the wheat — of those who
are of God and know they are of God and will defend
the right of God to aborn within them, to be born, to
come forth. Those who are not of God know they
are not of God and do not desire to perpetuate their
own seed, their own anti-God Self, and therefore are
the ones who have promoted abortion.

Policies of abortion

Beloved ones, those who are of the seed of the
murderer and the Liar from the beginning pursue
their policies of abortion simply because by nature
they are murderers. The question is then who

among the children of God have been indoctrinated by the Liar and his lie, and who among them are not the children of God but the wolves in sheep's clothing who have not the light of Christ in them, and therefore will never succumb to the great Logos, the great reason of the Word, that life is God from the moment of conception until the hour when the breath of the Holy Ghost returns to the Father and the crystal cord is cut and the threefold flame ascends to the etheric plane.

Beloved ones, those who deny life will not listen to reason. They will not accept facts and figures. And thus they stand exposed when you call forth the judgment and you bring the light of truth. Go not after these, then, but go after the lost sheep of the House of Israel who have lost their way through a false indoctrination and through the brainwashing of Zero Population Growth.

Go after the children of God who are making the karma and who ought to be liberated from the Liar and his lie. Draw them into the sheepfold. Give them the teaching and above all, the comfort of life.

Wolves in sheep's clothing

Crystal cord cut

False indoctrination
Brainwashing
Zero Population Growth

Comfort of life

Mother Mary

A Message — September 1972

The light you bear

The Light that shines this day in the dark streets of Jerusalem is the Light that you bear — the Light that you have carried here in the name of my Son, in the name of Christ Jesus, who also has walked with you these days. And as you have called to him, so he has said in your midst, "I and my Father are one." This oneness, blessed hearts of Light, is the one-ness which we share.

Throughout the ages people have always thought that their era was the modern time. Each successive decade considered itself to be more modern than the previous one, and so we say "in these modern times." Times have always been modern, for the modes of the human conscious-ness have changed little. You understand this — you who are the perceptive ones, who know that the Christ lives in all whom you meet, you who know that the Light must be borne in the physical octave that the physical octave might be healed by the power of the Divine Mother and the Divine Son.

Light borne in physical octave

The Light of God does not fail to raise up the human consciousness until it is brought to that level where it must either become divine or be con-

Raising of planet

sumed and be no more. The raising of the planetary body by the power of the Light of Christ — that cycle was begun in this very place in time and space, in this very forcefield two thousand years ago as the little band of the followers of the Light came together for that holy demonstration, the drama of eternity which was to portray the victory of the Light in every man, woman, and child.

The challenge of the two-thousand-year cycle which has followed has not been met by humanity. Heaven waits for the fulfillment of the cycle. There remain but a few short years of opportunity to become the Christ. And what will happen if mankind do not follow in His footsteps? I have prophesied before at Lourdes and Fatima and I shall prophesy again. For I have come to warn and to chastise and to urge men to pray the Our Father and to daily give the Rosary, for those to whom I spake understood the prayers that are necessary to sustain a momentum of Light.

Pray to Our Father daily give Rosary

Precious hearts, be not afraid; ye believe in me, believe also in Him. I am a cosmic mother, but this does not exclude yourselves; for you also are cosmic mothers and sons and daughters of God. And Jesus — was he not representing the Feminine Ray of the Divine Mother when he said, "O Jerusalem, Jerusalem ... how often would I have gathered thy children together, even as a hen gathereth her chicken under her wings, and ye would not." And so in the one who has attained the Christ Consciousness, there is the fourfold manifestation of the Father, the Mother, the Son, and the Holy Spirit in perfect alignment and in balance.

Alignment four lower bodies

The energies of this alignment of the four lower bodies with the divinity of the fourfold aspect of God's Consciousness — this mastery, this victory we have anchored in the physical octave in Jerusalem, in Bethlehem, in Bethany. Put off thy shoes from thy feet, for the place where thou standest is holy ground. Can you not also consecrate this ground? Can you not also consecrate the ground where you walk — wherever you walk, wherever you are in the world of form? This is your hour and this is your calling — to bring the Light and let it shine in the darkness of the streets of the cities of the world. This is the opportunity.

Light electrifying

The Light is a quickening power; it is electrifying. It leaps from heart to heart and from hearth to hearth. Be not discouraged, but bear a flaming sword that is the tenacity of an Archangel to press onward and onward and onward with courage unto the victory. Faint not; for the rainbow of promise is the path of attainment, of victory over the seven rays, of victory in the manifestation of the Christ-power, the Christ-love, the Christ-wisdom.

I say to you who have gathered here, there is much to be done. We who were gathered in the

Upper room

upper room, we who heard the teachings of the Master for forty days after his ascension — we know that only a handful of devotees chosen by the Lord

Beginning of 2000 year cycle

were responsible for beginning the cycle of two thousand years of Christendom, of the victory of the Light, of the victory of the Christ Consciousness and the culture of the Divine Mother.

Intensity of heart — victory

We know also that it is the intensity of the heart's devotion that determines the victory — not the quantity, not the numbers, not the numbers of people that can be herded into a gathering, into a church or a mosque. No, it is in the simplicity of the heart's devotion, the heart that has surrendered all unto Truth, unto victory, that is relentless in the search, in the quest, in the mission of leavening the entire lump of mankind's consciousness as the woman who took the leaven and hid it in three measures of meal and it leavened the entire lump of the mass consciousness.

I say to you, be that woman! Be the Divine Mother! Men and women of the Flame, I call to you to give mankind the victory by your individual devotion. Take the thoughts of the Holy Comforter and realize that they are a leaven, a yeast that expands when it is placed in the fertile dough of the minds of mankind. It expands and expands and expands almost involuntarily. The dough cannot

resist the yeast. The yeast takes over and it rises.
The dough rises, and so the consciousness of
mankind can be raised thusly.

Do you know, precious hearts, the angelic
hosts of Light who assisted in the releases of the
Brotherhood that have come to be known as the
Dead Sea Scrolls (the releases to the Essene
community) — those angelic hosts have watched
with great rejoicing as those same teachings which
have now been brought forth in The Everlasting
Gospel of God, *Climb the Highest Mountain,* have
been spread abroad in the hearts and minds of
those who are now reading that precious book.

The angelic hosts have watched as people
have accepted concepts in spite of themselves, in
spite of their resistance to Truth; for they have
followed the logic of the Divine Logos which
displaces, replaces, dissipates, and consumes the
logic of the carnal mind. And so, precious hearts,
when the minds and hearts of humanity are placed
upon the right track, the track that leads to God, it is
a resistless flow; it is an unceasing flow; it is a train
that never stops.

You have heard of the car of juggernaut which
represents mankind's karma and its descent at an
untimely moment. So I say to you, there is also a car
of the Christ-ideation, the action of the ideas of God
in the human consciousness which carry the de-
votee unto the victory by the very nature of the spiral
of God's Consciousness. And so the angels rejoice
that one, two, three, five, ten, one hundred, or a
thousand souls have been touched; for they become the leaven that shall leaven up the whole
lump. And so you are a part of that leaven — leaven
for the Christ, leaven for the Divine Mother.

Here is where it began two thousand years ago,
but it must begin again and again and again.
Wherever you stand, wherever you pray, wherever
you decree, there it begins again. A coil of Light is
spun. It whirls around and it widens; and each time it
whirls around, it gathers more of the chickens unto
the hen of the Divine Mother. Consider then the

Giant spiral of light

power of the Divine Logos as a giant spiral that goes out from you including greater and greater rings of Light, rings of humanity climbing upward on the spiral that you have begun by a right thought, a right word, a right deed.

Yes, you can go forward and portray the great drama in your own Jerusalem, in your own Bethlehem, in your own Bethany. For wherever you are, there God has sent you; and you cannot be where He has not called, where He Himself has not been.

Invoke your own Star

Be born again. Invoke your own Star — the Star of your mighty I AM Presence which shall become a Light which the shepherds and kings follow to the birthplace of the Christ over and over again. Fill the firmament of the heavens with stars so that mankind can follow them to the place of their own Divinity, the altar where the human consciousness is sacrificed for the Divine Consciousness and time is no longer and space is no longer, for all is one and eternity is now.

Be of good cheer, it is I. It is the I AM Presence within me, within you, within all, that is the Presence

Essene Brotherhood
Great White
Brotherhood

of your victory. On behalf of the Essene Brotherhood, a branch of the Great White Brotherhood, on behalf of the angels of Bethlehem, on behalf of the brothers and the sisters of my retreat, I offer to you my gratitude for your pilgrimage to the Holy Land and for your reconsecration of that land to the Flame of the Christ. In the name of the living God, who lives in all, I say, thank you.

Dictations reprinted by permission of Summit University Press. These dictations and others are available in cassette tapes and books, from Summit University Press, Box A, Malibu, California 90265, (213) 880-5300.

Chapter Notes — Research

Chapter 1/The Invisible War

1. *The World Almanac and Book of Facts, 1979* (New York: Newspaper Enterprise Association, 1978), p. 333. Total deaths (including battle and other casualties) for the Civil War were 780,213; World War I deaths totalled 320,710; and World War II deaths totalled 1,078,162.

2. Richard L. Walker, *The Human Cost of Communism in China,* prepared at the request of the late Senator Thomas J. Dodd, Chairman, Senate Subcommittee on Internal Security, Committee on the Judiciary, United States Senate (Washington, D.C.: ACU Education and Research Institute, January, 1977), pp. III-IV: Robert Conquest, famed British Sovietologist has calculated the total human cost of Soviet Communism to be somewhere between 35 million and 45 million lives; Professor Richard L. Walker, a lifetime student of Chinese affairs, estimates that communism in China, from the time of the first civil war (beginning in 1927), has cost a minimum of 34 million lives and that the total may run as high as 64 million lives. See also: Antony C. Sutton, *Wars and Revolutions: A Comprehensive List of Conflicts, Including Fatalities, Part One: 1820 to 1900* and *Part Two: 1900 to 1972* (Stanford University: Hoover Institute Press, 1971-1973).

3. "Scoreboard, 1978" *(American Opinion,* July-August, 1978), an annual update of a continuing assessment of individual nations' political and economic status, rates each nation on Earth between zero and one hundred percent, depending upon the extent to which ten criteria of a communist state (as outlined by Marx in Part II of the *Communist Manifesto,* "Proletarians and Communists") are currently in effect. The ten criteria are as follows:

(1) Abolition of property in land and application of all rents of land to public purposes.

(2) A heavy progressive or graduated income tax.

(3) Abolition of all right to inheritance.

(4) Confiscation of the property of all emigrants and rebels.

(5) Centralization of credit in the hands of the State, by means of a national bank with State capital and an exclusive monopoly.

(6) Centralization of the means of communication and transport in the hands of the State.

(7) Extension of factories and instruments of production owned by the State, the bringing into cultivation of waste lands, and the improvement of the soil generally in accordance with a common plan.

(8) Equal liability of all to labor. Establishment of industrial armies, especially for agriculture.

(9) Combination of agriculture with manufacturing industries; gradual abolition of the distinction between town and country by a more equable distribution of population over the country.

(10) Free education for all children in public schools. Abolition of children's factory labor in its present form. Combination of education with industrial production, etc., etc.

In 1978, the following countries were listed in the "Scoreboard" as being 90% or 100% communist, *i.e.*, nine or ten of the above criteria were in effect in that country as of May, 1978: Afars & Issas, Afghanistan, Albania, Algeria, Angola, Armenia, Azerbaidzhan, Benin, Bulgaria, Burma, Byelorussia, Cambodia, Cape Verde, Ceylon, Chad, Occupied China, Comoro Islands, Congo Republic, Cuba, Czecho-Slovakia, Equatorial Guinea, Estonia, Ethiopia, Finland, Georgia, East Germany, Guinea, Guinea-Bissau, Guyana, Hungary, Iceland, Iraq, Italy, Jamaica, Kazakh, Kenya, Kirghiz, North Korea, Laos, Latvia, Lebanon, Libya, Lithuania, Malagasy, Mali, Malta, Mauritius, Moldavia, Mozambique, Nepal, Niger, Outer Mongolia, Panama, Peru, Poland, Romania, San-Marino, Sao-Tome and Principe, Sierra Leone, Somalia, Soviet

Union, Syria, Tadzhik, Tanzania, Tibet, Trinidad & Tobago, Tunisia, Turkmen, Uganda, Ukraine, Uzbek, North Vietnam, South Vietnam, South Yemen, Yugoslavia, and Zambia.

4. John Barron and Anthony Paul, *Murder of a Gentle Land: The Untold Story of Communist Genocide in Cambodia* (New York: Reader's Digest Press, 1977), pp. 202-203.

U.S. newspapers carried reports such as the following: "[Since April 17, 1975], some 2.5 million of the previous eight million population have been executed outright or doomed to sure death when all cities and towns were ordered evacuated" *(Los Angeles Herald Examiner,* Oct. 5, 1977). Former President of Cambodia Lon Nol, having moved to Hawaii, also received information that 2.5 million Cambodians had been exterminated *(Rocky Mountain News,* Denver, Colo., Oct. 27, 1977).

5. The January 22, 1973 Supreme Court decision in *Roe v. Wade* held unconstitutional a Texas statute prohibiting all abortions except those necessary to preserve the mother's life. The Court included no comment or medical discussion on the life of the fetus. They simply stated, "We need not resolve the difficult question of when life begins. When those trained in the respective disciplines of medicine, philosophy, and theology are unable to arrive at any consensus, the judiciary, at this point in the development of man's knowledge, is not in a position to speculate as to the answer." The Court refused to go any further, or to comment on the 63 pages of evidence and the hundreds of experts who testified that life's beginning at conception is a foregone biological fact.

6. *World Population Growth and Response: 1965-1975, A Decade of Global Action* (Washington, D.C.: Population Reference Bureau, Inc.), p. 24: Even before

the Supreme Court decision in favor of abortion, John Robbins of the Planned Parenthood Federation of America estimated that "...more than 55 million women terminated their pregnancies by abortion — legal and illegal — during the year (1971), for a worldwide total of four (4) abortions for every ten (10) babies delivered." These caluculations were based on data from 87 countries included in the International Planned Parenthood Federation (IPPF) survey of 208 countries in 1971.

7. N.H. Mager and Jacques Kater, eds. *Conquest Without War* (New York: Trident Press, Simon-Schuster, 1961), p. 49. At Kremlin reception on November 26, 1956, Khruschev stated, "Whether you like it or not, history is on our side. We will bury you!"

8. W. Cleon Skousen, *The Naked Communist* (Salt Lake City, Utah: The Reviewer, 1962), pp. 290, 293; V.I. Lenin ("Report of the Central Committee at the 8th Party Congress," 1919): "The existence of the Soviet Republic side by side with imperialist states for a long time is unthinkable. One or the other must triumph in the end. And before that end supervenes, a series of frightful collisions between the Soviet Republic and the bourgeois states will be inevitable;" Dimitry Z. Manuilsky (a lecture at the Lenin School on Political Warfare in Moscow, 1931): "Today, of course we are not strong enough to attack...To win we shall need the element of surprise. The bourgeoisie will have to be put to sleep. So we shall begin by launching the most spectacular peace movement on record. There will be electrifying overtures and unheard of concessions. The capitalist countries, stupid and decadent, will rejoice to cooperate in their own destruction. They will jump at another chance to be friends. As soon as their guard is down, we shall smash them with our clenched fist."

Decades later, during a meeting in Moscow with six

U.S. senators, Soviet President Leonid Brezhnev "launched into a denunciation of his own 'belligerent' neighbors, the Chinese 'who speak of the inevitability of a new world war and oppose all efforts to prevent one.' 'It is too much,' he warned the American senators, 'to expect to be able to control China.' In a clear effort to make Washington think twice about trying to play off Moscow and Peking, he warned: 'If you put two bears in the ring, they might not fight each other. They may turn on you.' " ("A Talk with Brezhnev," Newsweek, January 22, 1979, pp. 41-42).

9. Antony C. Sutton, National Suicide: Military Aid to the Soviet Union (New Rochelle, N.Y.: Arlington House, 1973), p. 37. "This immoral dogma...was emphasized by Joseph Stalin: 'Words must have no relations to actions — otherwise what kind of diplomacy is it? Words are one thing, actions another. Good words are a mask for concealment of bad deeds. Sincere diplomacy is no more possible than dry water or wooden iron' (David J. Dallin, quoted in The Real Soviet Russia [New Haven: Yale University Press, 1971], p. 71).

Thus, it is not surprising that "A supressed report from British intelligence in early 1973 quoted Soviet leader Leonid Brezhnev as privately declaring that detente was a ruse designed to lead to a decisive shift in the balance of power" (The Boston Globe, February 11, 1977, p. 1). In this same meeting of East European Communist rulers, Brezhnev continued: "We are achieving with detente what our predecessors have been unable to achieve using the mailed fist...We have been able to accomplish more in a short time with detente than was done for years pursuing a confrontation policy with NATO... Trust us, comrades, for by 1985, as a consequence of what we are now achieving with detente, we will have achieved most of our objectives in Western Europe. We will have consolidated our position. We will have improved our economy. And a decisive shift in the correlation of forces will be such that, come 1985, we will be able to extend our will wherever we need to" ("Secret Speech: Did Brezhnev Come Clean?" *National Review,* Vol. 29, March 4, 1977, p. 250).

This same attitude was expressed as far back as 1919 by Zinoviev: "We are willing to sign an unfavorable peace. It would only mean we should put no trust whatever in the piece of paper we should sign. We should use the breathing space so obtained in order to gather our strength" *(Congressional Record)* Vol. 74, p. 7049, quoted in Sutton, *National Suicide,* p. 37). Which is exactly what has occured: "Meanwhile... the years of detente have coincided with the greatest military buildup in the history of nations... While Nixon and Kissinger traded away America's potential missile defense at SALT I, the Soviets have, in the intervening years, introduced whole new families of offensive weapons. For years the Brookings Institution used to produce an alternative budget showing how America could cut defense even deeper. Now, the scholars at Brookings are wondering aloud why the Soviets would continue to produce weapons when they have far more than conceivably needed for defense.

"All the while, as Soviet imperialism has become more naked and aggressive, as Soviet military power has eclipsed that of the West, there has flowed eastward a swollen stream of Western grain, technology, manufactured goods — much of it on comfortable credit terms which now total almost $50 billion to the East bloc" (Patrick J. Buchanan "In the Fifth Winter of Detente, Soviet Strength Is Still Growing," *Los Angeles Herald Examiner,* Dec. 19, 1978, p. A-14).

One of the Soviet Union's most important former political analysts and advisors for strategic arms limitation negotiations, Dr. Igor Glagolev, left his career at the top of the Disarmament Section of the Institute of World Economy and International Relations of the U.S.S.R. Academy of Science and managed to reach the United States. Taking a stand against the oppressive communist government that controls Russia, Glagolev has been briefing U.S. authorities on Soviet tactics to increase their strategic superiority over the U.S. He believes Soviet leaders will eventually be open about that superiority and use it to blackmail the Free World. "It is important that Americans understand this because, at the present time, a relatively small increase in U.S. defense spending for production of the delayed weapons, and for research, would close the gap and make such blackmail unlikely" (John Rees, "Former Soviet SALT Official Urges Us to Arm," *Review of the News,* May 10, 1978, pp. 31-42).

10. John M. Collins and Anthony H. Cordesman, *Imbalance of Power: Shifting U.S. Soviet Military Strengths,* A Report to the Senate Armed Services Committee (San Raphael, CA.: Presidio Press, 1978): Compared to the Soviet expenditure of 20% of their gross national product for defense, the U.S. commitment is only seven percent (7%) of our gross national product.

Whereas U.S. defense spending represented 64% of the federal budget in 1952, the $101.1 billion allocated for national defense in 1977 represented only 26% of the budget; when social security funds are included, the total Health, Education and Welfare [HEW] budget exceeds that of the Pentagon (Milton C. Cumming, Jr. and David Wise, *Democracy Under Pressure,* 3rd ed. [New York: Harcourt Brace Javanovich, 1977], p. 76). From 1966 to 1969, the Soviet total defense expenditures were only about 80% of the U.S. total defense costs; by 1975, however, the Soviet procurement had far surpassed the

U.S. outlay, equaling 182% of U.S. defense expenditures (Collins and Cordesman, *Imbalance of Power*).

11. *Phyllis Schlafly Report,* Vol. 11, No. 6, Section 1, January, 1978: "...the United States and other Western nations have loaned the U.S.S.R. and six Soviet satellites more than $49 billion since 1970. [These loans] are extremely hazardous because they are not secured by anything. There is no way to foreclose a loan to a Communist government. The Communist record for repaying loans is not inspiring. Russia paid back only about five percent of the $11 billion we loaned to it during World War II.

"The Soviet appetite for Western technology is staggering. The Soviets are gobbling up U.S. plans and plants as fast as they can, and our country is cooperating by sending free technical materials and factories and machines subsidized by longterm low-interest credits.

"The Soviets, for example, persuaded the United States to sell them an astronaut's space suit for $180,000. The space suit had cost the Americans $20 million to research and develop."

In an address to the Subcommittee VII of the Platform Committee of the Republican Convention at Miami Beach, Florida, August 15, 1972, Dr. Antony Sutton (then a Research Fellow at the Hoover Institute on War, Revolution and Peace, Stanford University) summarized: "Almost all [of Soviet technology] — perhaps 90-95 per cent — came directly or indirectly from the United States and its allies. In effect the United States and the NATO countries have built the Soviet Union — its industrial *and* its military capabilities. This massive construction job has taken 50 years, since the Revolution in 1917. It has been carried out through trade and the sale of plants, equipment and technical assistance." (Herman H. Dinsmore, *The Bleeding of America* [Belmont, Mass.: Western Islands, 1977]).

"The military potential of the industrial plants which we are building for the Soviets should be obvious to anyone. Trucks, aircraft, oil, steel, petrochemicals, aluminum, computers — these are the very sinews of a military-industrial complex. These factories, the product of American genius and financed by American capital, could have been built in the United States. Instead, they are constructed at the U.S. taxpayer's expense in the Soviet Union — a nation whose masters still keep millions in concentration camps and who have sworn to bury us. True, the 'Liberal' Establishment tells us that the Soviet leaders are only kidding when they tell their own people that they are accepting American aid in order to become strong enough to destroy us. But is is unlikely that Communist Party boss Leonid Brezhnev was jesting in June of 1971 when he declared in Moscow: 'There is no lull, there can be no lull, on the ideological front. That war continues and will continue until the complete victory of Communism...' As Professor Sutton observes: 'An American corporation may spend decades and millions of dollars developing a particular process or perfecting some new machine and then transfer it *en toto* to the Soviet Union." This research and development has taken place with tax-deductible dollars, once again leaving the American taxpayer to foot the bill for the looting." ("The Looters,"*American Opinion,* May, 1974, p. 12), See also: Sutton, *National Suicide.*

12. "An Intelligence Report,"*Review of the News,* Feb. 7, 1979, pp. 51-52. "Cuba has been supported not only by 'internationalist solidarity but also by American betrayal. In 1978 the Soviets installed in Cuba a ground-attack version of their Mig-23 aircraft, known as the Flogger. President Carter publicly defended this Soviet move, saying that the planes can no doubt carry nuclear weapons and drop them on the United States, but that 'whether the planes are outfitted to do so, designed to do

it, crews are trained to do it, is an entirely different matter and we don't have any indication that this is the case."

The map on the facing page shows that even during the year immediately following the Cuban Missile Crisis, contrary to their agreement with the U.S., the Soviet Union did not decrease their offensive missiles and troops in Cuba; the related article explains: "Since President Kennedy's lifting of the blockade on Cuba a year ago, Cuba has become an immense armed fortress. During the three months following the blockade 150,000 tons of arms were shipped to Cuba. The first six months of this year 429 Communist bloc ships and 205 Western vessles arrived in Cuba.

"The number of Soviet bloc troops, far from decreasing, has increased from 43,000 to 50,000, many of them wearing Castro army and militia uniforms and civilian clothes. Large numbers of arms, equipment, missiles, planes, and even an entire military base, are hidden in caves and underground installations" ("No Hay Nada De Nada," *Los Angeles Herald Examiner,* Oct. 20, 1963, p. F3).

13. "Soviet Record in 25 Summit Agreements," *U.S. News & World Report,* May 29, 1972, p. 29:

In seven summit meetings between a U.S. President and a Soviet leader, 25 agreements have been reached. The Soviets have violated 24 of those 25 agreements, according to a staff study for the Senate Judiciary Committee. Here is their record:

• 1943. At Teheran, in a meeting with British Prime Minister Winston Churchill and U.S. President Franklin D. Roosevelt, Joseph Stalin made four major agreements. Russia broke all of them.

• 1945. At Yalta, in another wartime Big Three meeting, Russia entered into six major agreements, of which five were violated. The only pledge kept was to enter the war against Japan — and that was done only after the outcome was decided.

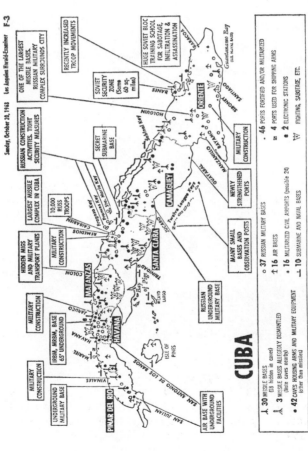

Sunday, October 20, 1963   Los Angeles Herald-Examiner   F-3

CUBA

UNDERGROUND MILITARY BASE — MILITARY CONSTRUCTION

MILITARY CONSTRUCTION

IRBM, MRBM, BASE 65' UNDERGROUND

HIDDEN MIGS AND MILITARY TRANSPORT PLANES

MILITARY CONSTRUCTION

LARGEST MISSILE COMPLEX IN CUBA

RUSSIAN CONSTRUCTION ACTIVITIES. TIGHT SECURITY MEASURES

RECENTLY INCREASED TROOP MOVEMENTS

ONE OF THE LARGEST MISSILE BASES. RUSSIAN MILITARY COMPLEX SURROUNDS CITY

HUGE SOVIET BLOC TRAINING SCHOOL FOR SABOTAGE, INFILTRATION & ASSASSINATION

SOVIET SECURITY ZONE (Some 60 sq. miles)

SECRET SUBMARINE BASE

10,000 RUSS TROOPS

MILITARY CONSTRUCTION

NEWLY STRENGTHENED PORTS

MANY SMALL BASES AND OBSERVATION POSTS

RUSSIAN UNDERGROUND MILITARY BASE

AIR BASE WITH UNDERGROUND FACILITIES

PINAR DEL RIO   HAVANA   MATANZAS   SANTA CLARA   CAMAGUEY   ORIENTE

ISLE OF PINES

Guantánamo Bay (U.S. NAVAL BASE)

30 MISSILE BASES (13 hidden in caves)

3 MISSILE BASES ALLEGEDLY DISMANTLED (Note caves nearby)

42 CAVES HOUSING ARMS AND MILITARY EQUIPMENT (other than missiles)

37 RUSSIAN MILITARY BASES

16 AIR BASES

16 MILITARIZED CIVIL AIRPORTS (possible 24)

10 SUBMARINE AND NAVAL BASES

46 PORTS FORTIFIED AND/OR MILITARIZED

4 PORTS USED FOR SHIPPING ARMS

2 ELECTRONIC STATIONS

FIGHTING, SABOTAGE, ETC.

INFORMATION in the map above refers only to some of the most important missile bases, Russian camps and caves with hidden arms. For example, in Oriente province only two caves are shown, whereas there reportedly are more than 50 caves in this province alone used to hold all types of armaments, including large numbers of 45-foot rockets with estimated range of 300 miles, claims Jose Norman.

• 1945. At Potsdam, where President Harry Truman represented U.S. in a summit meeting after Germany's surrender, Stalin made 14 major agreements. All were broken.

• 1955. At Geneva, in a Big Four meeting including France, Russia agreed that Germany's reunification problem should be settled by free elections. Moscow later refused to permit such elections.

No hard agreements were reached at the last three summit meetings — in 1959 when President Dwight Eisenhower met with Nikita Khrushchev in Camp David, Md.; in 1961 when President John F. Kennedy met with Khrushchev in Vienna, and in 1967, when Premier Alexei Kosygin conferred with President Lyndon B. Johnson in Glassboro, N.J.

The Russians similarly have failed to keep many other international agreements with the U.S. Examples:

• In World War II, the Soviets promised Western allies they were seeking no territorial aggrandizement. But Russia by 1948 controlled 11 countries — plus East Germany — and 750 million people.

• Russia repeatedly promised the U.S. between 1942 and 1946 that it would guarantee freedom and free elections in Hungary, Bulgaria, Poland, Czechoslovakia and Rumania. All those countries wound up with Communist dictatorships.

• The Kremlin pledged to repatriate World War II prisoners, but instead sent millions of them to slave labor camps.

• Russia gave the U.S. a promise that Korea would be free and independent — then set up a Communist government in the northern half of the country and masterminded an attempt to invade and conquer the rest of Korea. That broken promise cost the lives of 33,629 Americans.

- The Soviet Foreign Minister traveled to New York in 1946 and repeated a previous Kremlin promise that the Danube River would be opened to free navigation and trade. Today, the lower Danube, behind the Iron Curtain, is still a controlled Communist waterway.
- The Soviet Union promised the U.S. that it would treat Germany as one country after World War II — then sealed off its occupation zone, turned it into a separate country and is now seeking to make Germany's division permanent.
- Russia's promise of free travel between Berlin and the West has been broken repeatedly. Outstanding examples of this were the Berlin blockade of 1948-1949 and the 1961 construction of the Berlin Wall.
- Russia repeatedly assured the U.S. in 1962 that the arms build-up in Communist Cuba was purely defensive in character — then secretly put in offensive missiles aimed at the U.S. When this action was met by a firm U.S. challenge and naval blockade, Russia promised to remove the missiles.
- Faced with Russia's long history of breaking agreements, the U.S. attempted a tacit rather than a formal agreement to halt nuclear testing in 1958. In 1961 the Soviets broke this understanding and resumed testing.
- In signing a nonproliferation treaty in 1969, Russia promised to end the nuclear arms race and work toward disarmament. Instead, Russia accelerated its missile construction, overtook the U.S. and is now challenging in almost every category of nuclear weaponry.
- In 1970 Russia approved of a U.S. cease-fire plan in the Middle East, then helped Egypt violate it by moving SA-2 and SA-3 antiaircraft missiles up to the Suez Canal.

Other countries, as well as the U.S., have learned by experience that they could not rely on agreements with the Kremlin. Examples:

- In joining the League of Nations in 1934, Russia

pledged not to resort to war. In 1939, Russia was expelled from the League for acts of aggression, including the invasion of Poland and Finland — both countries with which Moscow had signed treaties of nonaggression.

• In violation of nonagression pacts, Russia invaded Estonia, Latvia and Lithuania in 1940 and incorporated them into the Soviet Union."

In an earlier study (1955), the staff of the U.S. Senate Committee on the Judiciary examined the Soviets' historical record of compliance with treaties. The committee staff "studied *nearly a thousand treaties* and agreements . . . both bilateral and multilateral, which the Soviets have entered into not only with the United States, but with countries all over the world. The staff found that in the 38 short years since the Soviet Union came into existence, its Government had broken its word to virtually every country to which it ever gave a signed promise . . . It keeps no international promises at all unless doing so is clearly advantageous to the Soviet Union. [We] seriously doubt whether during the whole history of civilization any great nation has ever made as perfidious a record as this in so short a time" (U.S. Senate, Committee on the Judiciary, *Soviet Political Agreements and Results,* 4th printing [Washington, 1964], quoted by Sutton in *National Suicide,* pp. 37-38).

14.   Zbigniew Brzezinski, *Between Two Ages: America's Role in the Technetronic Era* (Viking Press, 1970), pp. 258-259.

15.   Brzezinski, *Between Two Ages,* p. 72: "That is why Marxism represents a further vital and creative stage in the maturing of man's universal vision. Marxism is simultaneously a victory of the external, active man over the inner, passive man and a victory of reason over belief: it stresses man's capacity to shape his material destiny — finite and defined as man's only reality — and it

postulates the absolute capacity of man to truly understand his reality as a point of departure for his active
endeavors to shape it."

16. W. Cleon Skousen, *The Naked Communist* (Salt
Lake City, Utah: The Reviewer, 1968), pp. 69-72: "Marx
and Engels described religion as the opiate of the people
which is designed to lull them into humble submission
and an acceptance of the prevailing mode of production
which the dominant class desires to perpetuate . . . But it
was not the abuse of religion which Marx and Engels
deplored so much as the very existence of religion . . . It is
clearly evident from the numerous Communist writings
that what they fear in religion is not that it makes religious
people passive to the dominant class but that it *prevents*
them from becoming passive to Communist discipline.
Deep spiritual convictions stand like a wall of resistance
to challenge the teachings and practices of Communism . . .
        "As Anatole Lunarcharsky, the former Russian
Commissar of Education declared: 'We hate Christians
and Christianity. Even the best of them must be considered our worst enemies. They preach love of one's
neighbor and mercy, which is contrary to our principles.
*Christian love is an obstacle to the development of the
Revolution.* Down with love of our neighbor! What we
want is hate . . . Only then can we conquer the universe'
(quoted from the *U.S. Congressional Record,* Vol. 77,
pp. 1539-1540)."

17. Miles M. Costick, *Economics of Detente and
U.S.-Soviet Grain Trade* (Washington, D.C.: Heritage
Foundation, 1976), pp. 21-23: Since the early 1960's
several crop failures have forced Soviet leaders to
purchase high quantities of grain from foreign markets,
including millions of tons from the United States. In
hearings before the Permanent Subcommittee on Inves-
tigations, U.S. Senate *(Russian Grain Transactions,*

U.S. Government Printing Office, 1973), it became evident that "EKSPORTKHLEB, the Soviet grain agency, purposely exploited the weakness of a private economy by entering the U.S. market secretly, isolating the grain companies from one another, and therefore prevented the overall dimensions of the grain deal from being known ahead of time. In addition, the Commodity Credit Corporation (CCC) extended a credit of $750 million (of which $550 million was actually used) to the Soviet Union for imports of U.S. grain. The credit was extended for a three-year period, at interest rates of 6-1/8 percent. The U.S.D.A regulations at that time offered subsidies to any grain-purchasing nation, and the Soviets obtained large subsidies to enable them to continue buying wheat at the low price of about $1.59 a bushel. In effect, the inflationary impact of the grain sales and the government subsidies to the U.S.S.R. caused American tax-payers to pay twice for the purchases. American stock-piles were rapdidly depleted and the U.S. was unable to meet grain needs in underdeveloped areas, such as India, Bangladesh and Sub-Saharan Africa."

18. Costick, *Economics of Detente*, pp. 88-89: "According to Professor Raymond S. Steeper of the University of Tennessee's Space Institute and former Air Force Deputy Chief of Staff for Foreign Technology, Soviet war plans cover a wide range of both military and civilian activities.

" '[In 1964], a new civil defense manual was published in thousands of copies and distributed to all of the people in all of the [Russian] cities. Chapter 9 of this new manual describes how to build shelters for grain and food storage. At the same time, the new Soviet five-year plan — 1975 to 1980 — calls for over 1.5 billion bushels of grain. These storage sites are to be dispersed all over Russia near collective farms so that the people will have food in a nuclear war. This will clearly improve Soviet preparedness for nuclear war. It provides the finishing touches to perfect the war plans.'

"Professor Raymond Steeper suggests there is more involved than meets the eye in Soviet Union's need for more and more American grain."

19. Maj. Gen. George J. Keegan, Jr. (Ret.), *The Defense of America,* Summit University Forum lecture at Pasadena, California, Oct. 9, 1977 (tape album available from Summit University Press, Box A, Malibu, CA. 90265).

20. Keegan, *Defense of America.*

21. Keegan, *Defense of America.*

22. David A. Pietrusza, *Human Events,* May 26, 1979, p. 439; a book review of *The Eleventh Hour* by Gen. Lewis W. Walt, USMC (Ret.) (Ottawa, Il.: Caroline House). "As a former assistant commandant of the Marine Corps, Gen. Lew Walt is naturally most concerned with the sad state of America's once-proud defense capabilities . . .

" 'Wars are not lost, and national destinies not altered, only by weapons systems and the number of battalions under arms. They are forfeited long before that by a complicated series of decisions, fostered by a whole mind-set that fosters weakness and defeatism.'

"Yet the end result *is* military inferiority. In conventional forces the comparisons are staggering. Warsaw Pact forces outnumber NATO by 50,000 tanks to 10,000; 55,000 armored personnel carriers to 22,000; 22,000 artillery pieces to 5,000; 7,000 heavy mortars to 3,000. Our only strategy in Europe is to minimize our rout; the Soviet strategy is complete victory, planning for every eventuality. 'Soviet equipment is designed and built to fight on a battlefield that is contaminated with nuclear, chemical and biological agents,' says Walt, who has inspected Soviet arms captured by Israelis in the Yom Kippur War.

"We match the Russian juggernaut with an expensive, low-in-morale volunteer Army. Our bomber force relies on 316 ancient B-52s, the newest of which are 15 years old. The basic weapon of our infantryman, the M-16 .22 caliber rifle, is inferior to the Russian AK-47. Even our once invulnerable air power is questionable against Soviet capabilities. 'On March 4, 1978,' Gen. Robert J. Dixon, who was then chief of the Air Force's Tactical Air Command, was asked by a U.S. Senate committee if the American Air Force could succeed against the Soviet Air Force. His answer was a flat "No." '

"In even more deadly terms the Soviets outdeploy us in ICBMs 1,477 to 1,054. They have 82 missile-firing submarines with 909 missiles (even though they were allowed only 62 of these vessels under a Kissinger-negotiated arms pact) to our 41 submarines with 656 missiles. Moreover, these U.S. missiles have a range of only 2,800 miles; the Soviet range is 4,200 miles. Until recently our missiles were regarded as much more accurate. However, thanks to U.S. sales of high-precision ball bearings to the Soviet Union, we can no longer be so secure in this advantage."

Senator Jake Garn, a leader of opposition to the SALT II treaty, concurs that America's present military situation is inferior. He adds that "We simply can't afford to wait until the Soviets cheat to gear up our defenses. In the matter of sophisticated weaponry there is a long time-lag from drawing board to prototype to production line; and modern submarines, bombers, and missiles don't roll off the production line every few minutes like automobiles. For example, even though we have been working on the Trident submarine for several years it will be 1986 before the Trident program is operational.

"We have delayed making the decision on whether to go ahead with the MX mobile missile. Even if we decided to go ahead with it tomorrow, it would be 1986 or 1987 before those missiles were on the ground, shuttling between launch sites, and a credible deterrent.

"We don't have the time we used to have. People say, 'Oh, the United States can gear up just as we did after Pearl Harbor.' But we don't have months, or weeks, or even days" (John Rees, "Senator Jake Garn: The Leader Of Opposition to the SALT II Treaty in the Senate Tells How SALT Threatens Our Lives and Liberty," *Review of the News*, May 23, 1979, pp. 31-44).

23. See Antony C. Sutton, *War on Gold* (Seal Beach, Calif.: Seventy-Six Press, 1977).

24. See Kenneth C. Crowe, *America for Sale* (New York: Doubleday, 1978).

25. Robert Beck, one of a series of lectures on "Soviet Psychic Weaponry" presented at a convention of the International Cooperation Council, Pasadena, Calif., Jan. 24, 1979: In research on psychotronic radiation, conducted by the United States Psychotronics Society (founded by Henry Nagorka, Robert Beck, and Thomas Beardon), the most prevalent radiation (of low magnetic frequency) was consistently detected between the hours of three and four a.m.

26. Peter Tompkins and Christopher Bird, *The Secret Life of Plants* (New York: Harper and Row, 1973), pp. 161-178, 319-320. See also John Diamond, M.D., *Behavioral Kinesiology* (New York: Harper & Row, 1979).

27. According to the 1978 *Statistical Abstracts of the United States*, 99th Annual Edition (Washington, D.C.: U.S. Department of Commerce, Bureau of the Census, Government Printing Office), p. 124: Over 46 million people in the United States were cigarette smokers in 1976.

28. See William Dufty, *Sugar Blues* (New York: Warner Books, 1975).

29. See Gladys Caldwell and Philip E. Zanfagna, M.D., *Fluoridation and Truth Decay* (Reseda, Calif.: Top-Ecol Press, 1974); and *Fluoridation of Water,* Hearings Before the Committee on Interstate and Foreign Commerce, House of Representatives, Eighty-third Congress, Second Session, on H.R. 2341, A Bill to Protect the Public Health from the Dangers of Fluoridation of Water, May 25, 26, and 27, 1954.

On Mar. 29, 1957, in the State of Colorado, County of Arapahoe, a notorized deposition was given by Oliver Kenneth Goff, who was a member of the Communist Party and the Young Communist League from May 2, 1936 to Oct. 9, 1939. His testimony before the Government is incorporated in Vol. 9 of the Un-American Activities Report for the year 1939. While a member of the Communist Party, he attended Communist underground training schools outside the city of New York and in Milwaukee, Wisc. There they were trained in the art of revolutionary overthrow of the established Government. "We discussed quite thoroughly the fluoridation of water supplies and how we were using it in Russia as a tranquilizer in the prison camps. The leaders of our school felt that if it could be induced into the American water supply, it would bring about a spirit of lethargy in the nation; where it would keep the general public docile during a steady encroachment of Communism. We also discussed the fact that keeping a store of deadly fluoride near the water reservoir would be advantageous during the time of the revolution, as it would give us opportunity to dump this poison into the water supply and either kill off the poulace or threaten them with liquidation, so that they would surrender to obtain fresh water... [It] was felt by the leadership, that if a program of fluoriding the water could be carried out in the nation, it would go a long way toward the advancement of the revolution."

Despite all evidence to the contrary, the American Dental Association (ADA) still recommends the use of fluoride by the public; it even advises pregnant women living in areas where the water supply contains less than 1 ppm of fluoride to take fluoride supplements *(Accepted Therapeutic Manual* [Chicago: Council on Dental Therapeutics of the ADA, Jan. 1979)]

30. See John Barron, *The KGB: The Secret Work of Soviet Secret Agents* (New York: Readers Digest Press, 1974, pp. 12-13).

31. See Sutton, *National Suicide,* "U.S. Assistance for Soviet Military Computers," pp. 205-209.

"The February 7, 1978 issue of the Soviet newspaper *Red Star* carried an interview with the commander of the Soviet Navy, Admiral Sergei Gorshkov, in which he states that the development of nuclear and computer technology has made it possible for the Soviets to build warships that more than meet the requirements of present-day warfare. He was talking about Soviet military development based upon *American* technology.

"Soviet physicist Andrei Sakharov has commented: 'In the 1920s and 1930s...the slogan "Catch up with and surpass America" was launched, and we really were catching up for several decades' because of massive U.S. shipments of technology. 'Then the situation changed. The second industrial (computer) revolution began and now in the 1970s we can see that rather than catching up with America, we are falling farther behind...'

"Moscow has been trying to overcome this technological backwardness by begging, buying, and stealing technology from the West" (Daniel J. Sobieski, "America's Computer Sellout," *American Opinion,* April 1979, pp. 23-24).

In an article entitled "The Great Bleep Forward," *Time* of July 16, 1973, quoted Wade Holland, editor of Rand Corporation's *Soviet Cybernetics Review,* as stating: "The Soviet computer industry has always been a shambles." Later, *Time* continued: "Control Data Corp. has delivered the largest Western machine in the Soviet

Union, a Model 6200 now at the Dubna Research
Institute; the company is negotiating the setting up of a
time-sharing network in Russia... In the past, the U.S.
Government has blocked sales of many high-
technology items like computers to the Soviet Union if it
appeared that national defense might be compromised"
(quoted in *American Opinion,* May 1974, pp. 10-11).

"In 1965 only five thousand dollars' worth of elec-
tronics components and parts were directly shipped
from Washington to Moscow, and only two thousand
dollars" worth in 1966. In 1967 computer exports increased to one million dollars. By 1969, thanks to the
Kissinger *detente,* it was estimated that Western computer sales to all of the Warsaw Pact was running at forty
million dollars annually, in great part from European
subsidiaries of American companies. In the past four
years, however, U.S. computer manufacturers have sold
to the U.S.S.R. and its satellites over three hundred
million dollars' worth of computers and related equipment" (Sobieski, p. 91).

32. Matt. 7:16, 20.

33. *Bhajans: Devotional Songs with the Chelas of
Guru Ma* (Los Angeles: Summit University Press, 1977),
p. 14: "Many of the symbolic elements surrounding the
mission of Jesus Christ directly relate to the tales told of
Krsna [Krishna]. Both were born to establish religions of
love through the wisdom of the Great Lawgiver and were,
indeed, Love incarnate. Both were raised in simple
homes and both were a threat to the reigning temporal
power and his rule of darkness. The story goes that the
cruel king Kamsa was told by a seer that his sister,
Devaki, would give birth to a son who would assassinate
him. He had her first six children killed, the seventh
escaped, and the eighth was Krsna. He was born in the
palace at midnight. He was the jewel of the Raghu race —
dark-skinned and radiant. His life was greatly en-

dangered, but the gods intervened to save the life of the avatar. The guards of the palace were induced with a heavy sleep and Vasu-deva, Krsna's father, escaped with the child. He exchanged Krsna for the daughter of a cowherd named Nanda. When Kamsa discovered the trickery, he ordered that every male child be killed — just as Herod had done. Nanda, alert to his responsibility, quickly moved his family away from the city to Gokula, as Joseph took Mother and child and fled to Egypt."

Ex. 1:8 through 2:10 describes the similar experience of Moses, whose life was threatened by the king of Egypt's order that all male babies be killed.

34. Population Reference Bureau, *World Population Growth and Response*, p. 24.

35. Mary Lewis Coakley, *Rated X: The Moral Case Against TV* (New Rochelle, N.Y.: Arlington House, 1977): An average child views 18,000 TV murders before he graduates from high school. See also: Marie Winn, *The Plug-In Drug* (New York: Viking Press, 1977), pp. 73-84.

36. See "TV's Effect: From Alpha to Z-z-z . . ," an article about research by sociologist Herbert Krugman, in the *Los Angeles Times*, Mar. 11, 1979, pp. 1-29. See also Winn, *The Plug-In Drug*, pp. 40-47.

37. Peggy Mann, "The Case Against Marijuana,"*Family Circle*, Feb. 20, 1979, pp. 22-103: Robert L. DuPont, former director of the National Institute on Drug Abuse, stated for this article that "While Americans were debating the question of criminal penalties for marijuana possession, the real tragedy has overtaken us almost unnoticed: the alarming levels of very high marijuana use among our young people. For all practical purposes, decriminalization took place several years ago, and nowhere in this country are more than a handful of people in prison because of marijuana possession. The

real issue is the *health danger posed by this epidemic ...*"

In another article, Ms. Mann continues: " 'The full range of these consequences' is now starting to come clear. Recently, at the medical school in Reims, France, 41 scientists from 13 nations presented new research findings linking the use of marijuana with harmful effects on human reproduction, the brain and other body cells, including the lungs" (Peggy Mann, "Say It Isn't So — There's Bad News About Marijuana," *Los Angleles Times,* Aug. 6, 1978, p. V-3; this article first appeared in the *Washington Post).*

Despite the hazards of its usage, marijuana has never been more prevalent nor more accepted in the United States: "An estimated 16 million Americans use marijuana. In fact, according to *Human Behavior* magazine, the sale of marijuana — 48 billion dollars' worth in 1977 — is the third biggest business enterprise in the U.S., behind only General Motors and Exxon. The weed is also reportedly the nation's second leading import measured in dollar volume, topped only by passenger cars" *(Review of the News,* Dec. 6, 1978).

"A 19-year-old University of California sophomore is the happy winner of a marijuana raffle that netted her a kilo of what the sponsors described as 'fairly decent Colombian' grass.

"She said in a telephone interview after the raffle she will use the marijuana, valued at $2,000 on the illegal market, to keep her friends 'happy and smoking.'

" ... The raffle was sponsored by a group supporting a marijuana initiative on the ballot in Tuesday's Berkeley municipal election.

"The drawing was conducted in Wheeler Auditorium on the UC campus. Campus police did not interfere. The sponsors previously conducted a 'smoke-in' on campus, and there were no arrests.

"Asked whether she would inform her parents about the marijuana, she said: 'Of course. They won't like the prize, but they'll be very happy that I won" (United Press International, "Student Wins $2,000 'Pot' " *Los Angeles Times,* Feb. 1979).

38. "Religion in America," *The Gallop Opinion Poll Index,* 1977-1978.

39. See John W. Whitehead. *The Separation Illusion: A Lawyer Examines the First Amendment* (Milford, Mich.: Mott Media, 1977), especially pp. 95-124.

40. 1 Tim. 4:2.

41. See Herbert Hendin, *The Age of Sensation* (New York: Norton, 1975).

Chapter 2/Coming of the Avatars

1. *1975 Yearbook of Science and the Future* (Chicago: Encyclopaedia Britannica, 1974), pp. 181-183, and Griffith Park Observatory, Public Information, Los Angeles: Comet Kohoutek was discovered by astronomer Lubos Kohoutek on a photograph taken Mar. 7, 1973 at Hamburg Observatory in West Germany. As Kohoutek moved from the constellation Hydra toward our sun, it became visible to the naked eye by late November, with a tail visible by December 18. At the time of the perihelion (the point of its orbit nearest our sun), Kohoutek was not visible to people on Earth, but was photographed by the U.S. satellite OSO-7, as a brilliant blob superimposed on the solar corona. The first comet to be observed at radio wavelengths, Kohoutek was surrounded — when near the sun — by an enormous halo of glowing hydrogen gas, detectable only in ultraviolet light.

See text of dictation by Maitreya (Oct. 1973) in Part III, "The Prophecy Incarnate."

2. Gen. 37:3; Joseph's coat refers to the soul's mastery of

the seven rays of Christic light, reflected in the aura as a
shimmering fountain of light — a sign of attainment.

3. See full text of dictation by Lady Master Venus (Feb. 4,
1962) in Part III, "The Prophecy Incarnate."

Chapter 3/Schoolroom of the Soul

1. Acts 9:18.

Chapter 4/Ascent and Descent

1. See Richard D. Bach, *Jonathan Livingston Seagull:
A Story* (New York: Macmillan Co., 1970).

2. See illustrations in Djwal Kul, *Intermediate Studies of
the Human Aura* (Los Angeles: Summit University
Press, 1974).

3. Wilson Bryan Keye, *Subliminal Seduction* (New
York: Signet Books, New American Library, 1973), including illustrations.

Chapter 5/Law of Karmic Return

1. Gen. 9:6. See also Gal. 6:7, "Be not deceived; God is
mocked: for whatsoever a man soweth, that shall he also
reap."

2. Mark and Elizabeth Prophet, *Climb the Highest
Mountain* (Los Angeles: Summit University Press, 1972),
pp. 75-76, 399.

3. Abraham Lincoln's Second Inaugural Address, delivered on March 4, 1865.

4. Matt. 3:3, Mark 1:3, Luke 3:4, John 1:23.

5. See text of dictation by Archangel Zadkiel in Part III, "The Prophecy Incarnate."

6. Dr. Brohmuil Stipul, Czechoslovakia's Deputy Minister of Health, stated, "Roughly 25% of the women who interrupt their first pregnancy have remained permanently childless;" quoted in *Handbook on Abortion* by Dr. and Mrs. J.C. Wilkie, rev. ed. (Cincinnati, Ohio: Hayes Co., 1979), p. 93. Other physical complications experienced by these women are cited by the Wilkies in Chap. 11, pp. 89-97.

7. Ex. 7:17-20

8. Rev. 16:4, "And the third angel poured out his vial upon the rivers and fountains of waters; and they became blood."

9. Rev. 20:14, "And death and hell were cast into the lake of fire. This is the second death." Rev. 21:8, "But the fearful, and unbelieving, and the unabominable, and murderers, and whoremongers, and sorcerers, and idolaters, and all liars, shall have their part in the lake which burneth with fire and brimstone: which is the second death."

Chapter 6/Veil of Ignorant Bliss

1. The following resources document and elaborate upon the information presented in Chapter 6:
(a) Agneta Philipson, L.D. Sabath, and David Charles, "Transplacental Passage of Erythromycin and Clindamycin," *New England Journal of Medicine,* vol. 2, no. 23 (June 1973), p. 1219.
(b) Antti Vaheri *et al,* "Isolation of Attenuated Rubella-Vaccine Virus from Human Products of Conception

and Uterine Cervix," *New England Journal of Medicine,* vol. 286, no. 20 (May 1972), p. 1072

(c) Peter A.J. Adam, *et al,* "Human Placental Barrier to 121I-Glucagon Early in Gestation,"*Journal of Clinical Endocrinology and Metabolism,* vol. 34 (May 1972), pp. 772-782.

(d) Victor Cohn,"Scientists and Fetus Research,"*Washington Post,* April 15, 1973.

(e) Bob Wyrik, "100 Fetuses Used in Tests for Insecticides,"*Sacramento Bee,* July 28, 1977.

(f) John E. Harrington, MSW, "Experimentation with Prenatal and Neonatal Human Beings," pts. 1-2, *Marriage and Family Newsletter,* vol. 3, nos. 1-2 (Jan.-Feb., 1972).

(g) Paul H. Mussen, ed., *Carmichael's Manual of Child Psychology,* 3rd ed. (New York: Wiley, 1970), pp. 507, 510-511, 513.

(h) S.S. Stevens, *Handbook of Experimental Psychology* (New York: Wiley, 1958), pp. 285-286.

(i) Diana Copsey and Marion Gold, "NIH Ethics Policy Near on Fetal Research," *Ob. Gyn. News,* April 15, 1973.

(j) *National Observer,* April 21, 1973.

(k) Paul Ramsey, *The Ethics of Fetal Research* (New Haven: Yale University Press, 1975), pp. 6-7.

(l) *Federal Register,* vol. 39, no. 165 (Aug. 1974), pp. 30648-30657.

(m)*Federal Register,* vol. 40, no. 154 (Aug. 1975), p. 33530.

(n) Juliana G. Pilon, "Semantic Problems of Fetal Research,"*Human Life Review,* vol. 2, no. 3 (Summer 1976), pp. 93-94.

(o) Arthur J. Moss, M.D., *et al,* "Blood Pressure and Vasomotor Reflexes in the Newborn Infant,"*Pediatrics,* vol. 32, no. 2 (August 1963), pp. 175-176.

(p) Forrest H. Adams, M.D. and John Lind, M.D., "Physiologic Studies on the Cardiovascular Status of Normal Newborn Infants (with Special Reference

to the Ductus Arteriosus),"*Pediatrics,* vol. 19, no. 3 (March 1957), p. 434.
 (q) Nick Thimmesch, "Life is Cheap to Many Doctors, Lawmakers,"*Newsweek,* July 9, 1973. Thimmesch was citing Dr. Franz Ingelfinger from the *New England Journal of Medicine,* vol. 288 (April 1973), pp. 791-792.

2. Litchfield and Kentish, *Babies for Burning,* p. 39.

Chapter 7/Soul Identity and Polarity

1. William Shakespeare; spoken by the character 'Jaques' in *As You Like It.*

2. Elizabeth Clare Prophet, "Your Marriage Made On Earth," *Family Designs for the Golden Age,* a seminar presented June 15, 1974 (tape album available from Summit University Press, Box A, Malibu, CA 90265).

3. Rev. 14:15, Peter 2:22, John 14:30.

4. Elizabeth Clare Prophet, Lecture in New Orleans on Feb. 24, 1978.

5. Author's note: The three energies of the kundalini which flow from the base chakra, the Mother chakra, are the ida, sushuma and pingala. When the Kundalini is opened and it begins to rise, it is an action of the threefold light that's in the heart, but it isn't a flame; it's a flow of the Mother energy. The sushuma is in the center of the spinal column; the ida and pingala are on the outside. So it's the Father and Mother — Alpha and Omega — on the outside and the Christ energies in the center. When either the Alpha or Omega energy is weakened, throwing the energies out of balance, the ascension flame cannot rise.

6. See Dr. Thelma Moss. *The Probability of the Impossible: Scientific Discoveries and Explorations in the Psychic World* (Los Angeles: J.P. Tarcher, 1974), especially Chap. 2, pp. 23-61.

7. See Alfred J. Toynbee, *A Study of History: The Disintegration of Civilization,* Vol. 1-12 (London: Oxford University Press, 1947-1954).

8. Luke 23:29

9. See Amazonia, "The Culture of the Mother Race," a dictation given Dec. 16, 1962, *Pearls of Wisdom (1978),* Vol. 21, Nos. 18-19, pp. 87-94.

Chapter 8/Marriage, a Soul Initiation

1. See Mark and Elizabeth Prophet, *Climb the Highest Mountain,* p. 410. Also available from Summit University Press (Box A, Malibu, CA 90265) are tape albums of seminars: *Family Designs for the Golden Age* (1974), and *Twin Flames in Love, I* (1978).

2. John 14:12.

3. Comments by Elizabeth Clare Prophet, in conference with the author, Dr. Yaney.

Chapter 9/Role of Sex

1. Gen. 3:4.

2. Gen. 2:9.

3. Gen. 3:16

4. See dictation by Maitreya in Part III, "The Prophecy Incarnate."

5. Is. 41:23

6. Hab. 1:13, *"Thou art* of purer eyes than to behold evil, and canst not look on iniquity..."

Chapter 10/Man Transcending Himself

1. John 14:12.

2. Archangel Raphael, *Pearls of Wisdom,* vol. 10, no. 45, (Nov. 5, 1967):
"...Because the role of the mother is vital in the creation of Opportunity for the incoming Soul, there is a particular desire in My Heart to place in the hands of all prospective mothers, and those who have among their friends mothers who desire to behold Good rather than evil, information of a scientific nature concerning the bearing of God's children, in order that they might live in the Essence of Good and remain uninfluenced by the evils of the world... [The] Laws of the Spirit which were employed so beautifully by Mary when she carried the founding Christ in Her Womb remain as new as time and eternity. Today, as always, the application of these Laws can draw, unto mothers who wish to learn to love, that full measure of devotion which will provide an avenue of Comfort to the incoming child as well as the resurgence of its latent spiritual nature, its benign intelligence and its emotional control. ...We urge both mother and father to contemplate the beautiful in art, in literature, in drama, in nature and in relationships between peoples so that the young child that is growing within may be imbued with the best Gifts in Life. It is not enough to let him inherit your bones or the chemistry of your blood, nor would it be enough, though you were charged with spirituality, to

give him but your own measure thereof. Seek, rather, to draw from the Godhead, from the Star of the Soul that shines above, awaiting the moment of birth, the Substance that only the Angel that dwells in the Presence of God can give...

Dwell not, then, in the world of illusion, in the jungle of tangled emotions, in the sense barrier of separation from the Invisible Realm. Let thy thoughts, the thoughts of thy heart and mind reach right through; for We will smile through every cloud of worldly substance if you will inspire in your heart to be that wonderful mother that Mary was..."

3. "Memory Transfer Experiments," research conducted since 1957 by the Department of Psychology at the University of Michigan (funded by the Atomic Energy Commission and the National Institutes of Mental Health): Flatworms which had been trained to respond to electrical stimuli with certain behavior (in a maze) were ground up and fed to other flatworms. The new flatworms exhibited the same trained behavior, thereby suggesting that there had been a chemical transfer, probably via cytoplasmic substance, including RNA.

Chapter 11/Raising of the Planet

1. A study by the North American Newspaper Alliance (N.A.N.A.), quoted in *Review of the News,* Feb. 25, 1976, p. 59, reveals that an estimated 71 million people receive government assistance, including Social Security and Welfare. [This represents one third of the U.S. population and is larger than our working force.]

2. Bureau of the Census, *1978 Statistical Abstracts,* p. 147.

3. Congressman Eldon Rudd, Ariz., quoting Statistics

compiled by the Department of Commerce; *Review of the News,* July 5, 1978, p. 59: Excluding both inflation and the cost of government regulation, 47¢ of every dollar earned in the United States goes to the government for taxes at all levels. See also Gary Allen, *Tax Target: Washington* (Seal Beach, Calif.: 76 Press, 1978), p. 132.

4. "Religion in America," *1977-78 Gallop Opinion Index,* pp. 41-43: 34% of Americans say they have been "born again."

5. "Religion in America," *1977-78 Gallop Opinion Index,* p. 17.

6. Bureau of the Census, *1978 Statistical Abstracts.* Also, a new Census Bureau report shows that the United States had about 5.5 million fewer children under age 17 in 1977 than it did in 1970; the under-5 population has decreased nearly 2 million, or 11.2% since 1970, and the school-age population, ages 5 to 17, dropped 3.5 million (Associated Press, *Los Angeles Times,* Feb. 1979).

7. Rev. Fr. V. Montes De Oca, C.S.Sp., *More About Fatima and the Immaculate Heart of Mary,* trans. Rev. J. Dacruz, C.S.Sp. (Castelbranco), (Potts Point, Australia: Apostles of Mary, 1974) and Emmett Culligan, *The 1960 Fatima Secret* (Rockford, Ill.: Tan Books, 1975). Mother Mary gave much instruction during her appearances to the children of Fatima. Most of this teaching — such as her admonition to daily give the rosary, to obtain peace for the world — was immediately released to the general public. Mother Mary specified, however, that one part of the message was to be held by hierarchy of the Roman Catholic Church until 1960, then given to the world. In 1960, contrary to expectations, Pope John XXIII did not reveal the secret to the world. Later, Pope Paul VI allowed certain diplomats in Washington, London and Moscow, including Nikita Kruschev and John F. Kennedy, to see

part of the message. A copy of a letter purported to be the secret (originally written down by one of the children and delivered by her bishop to the Holy See in 1954) was printed in the Stuttegart, Germany newspaper, *Neues Europa,* on Oct. 15, 1963, and again in the Paris, France paper, *Le Monde et la Vie,* in Sept. 1964:

"Do not be troubled, dear child, I am the Mother of God who is speaking to you and begging you to announce the following message to the entire world in my name: Good people must be better. They must implore God to forgive the sins they have committed and will in the future commit. A great chastisement will come over all mankind — not today or tomorrow but in the second half of the twentieth century. Humanity has been sacreligious and has trampled under foot the wondrous blessings of God. No longer does order reign anywhere, even in the highest places Satan reigns and directs the course of things. Satan will even succeed in infiltrating into the highest positions in the Church. Satan will succeed in sowing confusion in the minds of the scientists who design weapons that can destroy great portions of mankind in short periods. Satan will gain hold of the heads of nations and will cause these destructive weapons to be mass produced. If mankind will not oppose these evils, I will be obliged to let the arm of my son drop in vengeance. If the chief rulers of the world and the Church will not actively oppose these evils, I will ask God my Father to bring his justice to bear on mankind. Then will God punish mankind even more severely and heavily than he did at the time of the great deluge. But a time of very severe trial is also coming for the Church. Cardinals will oppose cardinals and bishops will oppose bishops. Satan will enter into their very midst and will walk in their ranks. In Rome also will occur great changes — what is rotten will fall and what falls must not be retained. The Church will be obscured and all the world will be thrown into great confusion. The great, great war will come in the second half of the twentieth century. Fire and smoke will drop from heaven and the waters of the ocean will turn to steam throwing their foam to the very sky. Whatever is standing will be overturned. Millions of people will die. Those surviving will envy the dead. Distress, misery, and desolation will be found the world over. The time is drawing nearer and the abyss is ever deepening and there will be no escape. The great and powerful will perish with the lowly and meek. The good will die with the wicked, the princes of the Church with their faithful and the rulers of nations with their people. Death will reign everywhere raised to triumph by erring men. The helpers of Satan will be the masters of the earth. These evils will come at a time when no one expects it. Nevertheless it must come as punishment and revenge in accordance with God's plan. Later however, God in his glory will once more be invoked and will once more be served as he was not so long ago when the world had not yet been corrupted. The time of times is come, the end of all ends, if mankind is not converted. Woe! Woe if that conversion does not come about and if everything remains as it is now or worsens. Call upon all true followers of my son Jesus Christ to go and announce this for I will always be at your side to assist you."

An example of the power of the rosary was cited Oct. 27, 1977 in an article about Schuyler Falls, N.Y. in *The Wanderer* (St. Paul, Minn):

"Both abortion clinics in this small upstate New York town have been closed after three and one-half years of weekend operations and over 5,000 acknowledged abortions. Town Clerk Donald Dashnaw attributes the closures to prayers and petitions to the Mother of God over a 17-month period. ..."One dozen 'out-of-town' doctors have admitted practicing abortion in Schuyler Falls with as many as five different practitioners ploying their trade in as many weekends. The flood of business was so rushed that preliminary hearings, called by the State of New York Department of Health, cite improper and incomplete filing of certificates, alleging violations which call for fines or imprisonment ... [However, the] violations of improper filings ... are unlikely to result in fines of major consequence — that is to say, enough to suspend any doctor from further practice. Nor does Town Clerk Dashnaw contend that the perseverence of his office in bringing to light the wrongs ... is the major reason for the closing. [Rather], Dashnaw attributes the recent town's reprieve from infanticide to prayers and petitions to the Mother of God.

"Commencing in February, 1976, a concerted effort was made in Clinton County to promote the Fatima Message and the Rosary. The Town Clerk became part of their effort praying along with others that through intercession the blight of abortion would leave Schuyler Falls. From February, 1976, to the closing of the two offices in June, 1977, these following Marian events took place in Clinton County: ...the Fatima Message was given in talks by Dashnaw at 75 Masses in 23 Churches of Clinton County. The Fatima Pilgrim Virgin Statue visited 27 homes (a week at a time). ...All these visits resulted in Family Enthronement Masses dedicated to the Sacred Heart. At least four Parish Blue Army Cells were started with the aim of Rosary recitation weekly by family units. ...In the summer and fall of 1976, the Blue Army of Clinton County set up booths at the County Fair and local shopping plaza. ...[The] Knights of Columbus Council ... established a unit of "Men of the Sacred Heart" which is continuing to bring the Fatima Pilgrim Statue to area homes. Finally, the world-travelled "International Pilgrim Virgin Statue" visited Clinton County for the second time within one year. Appropriately, the second visit culminated in a reparation and thanksgiving service just a few hundred yards from the closed abortion clinics.

"The pleadings to Mary seem not to have gone in vain. The Town Clerk reasons that the Blessed Mother played the major role in the recent victory in Schuyler Falls."

Chapter 12/Turning of the Cycles

1. Rev. 6:16.

2. Cor. 6:17, "Wherefore come out from among them, and be ye separate, saith the Lord, and touch not the unclean *thing;* and I will receive you."

De. 7:6, "For thou *art* an holy people unto the Lord thy God: the Lord thy God hath chosen thee to be a special people unto himself, above all people that *are* upon the face of the earth."

Also see dictation by Archangel Uriel in Part III, "The Prophecy Incarnate."

Part III/The Prophecy Incarnate

1. See *Prayer and Meditation* (Los Angeles: Summit University Press, 1978), Chapter 26, pp. 246-253.

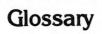

Glossary

10,001. Advanced souls of great light, Avatars, volunteering to come to Terra earth, embodying now from the etheric retreats and cities of light, as prophesied by Lord Maitreya. They come from other systems of worlds and have never before embodied on Terra, until the present hour. They are revealed in code in the book of Revelation as "a great wonder in heaven." (Rev. 12:2)

144,000. Represents advanced souls of light, also known as the twelve tribes of Israel (Gen. 49:28; Rev. 21:12), who volunteered to descend into the dark, dense planet earth with Sanat Kumara, and accompanied him as his retinue to assist him in the evolution of the lifewaves entrapped in the darkness of the planet. The first of this group to come forward out of the darkness was Gautama Buddha, setting the path of light — of initiation for souls to return; and the second was Buddha Maitreya.

Ascension. A ritual on the inner planes of mastery over time and space, a change of frequency of the soul, no longer needing to balance karma in the physical plane, ascending to another plane of soul existence in a changed, permanent light body. Jesus visibly demonstrated this path to those closest to him, an advanced initiation for those who were permitted the experience of observing his victory.

Aura. A light forcefield surrounding and interpenetrating the physical body, a radiation of light of different wavelengths and frequencies covering some of the visible spectrum of the human eye and the invisible spectrum of the third eye and the etheric plane. This invisible spectrum is, however, visible to advanced, evolved souls with highly developed etheric vision. Modern science has not yet perfected a sensitive instrument capable of measuring this vibratory frequency. There are, however, some primitive instruments similar to dowser instruments that can outline the auric field.

Kirlian photography utilizes a high-voltage radio frequency to assist in the outlining of the aura for photography and is considered to be also a very primitive method of measurement. It is thought that the radiating energy of the aura originates from the fire and the light in the core of the atom and that this light can be intensified at will through a proper alignment of the universal energy source of the God-presence. The luminous light surrounding advanced souls and caught by the ancient Renaissance painters is a visible portrayal of this radiation of light.

Chakras. There are seven major chakras vertically aligned along the spine, and a total of 144 of these energy centers at various points of the human body that are associated with accupressure points known to the healing arts.

Court of the Sacred Fire. The court and the lake of fire spoken of in the Bible in the book of Revelation (Rev. 20:14-15) is an august body of elders of God known as the Four and Twenty Elders (Rev. 4:4) who sit in judgment of soul lifestreams as they pass for review when their cycles of time for evolution are complete and the records of their lifestreams are unsealed by the Angel of Record and the Keeper of the Scrolls. A soul with a positive record weighed in the scales of light and darkness, a cosmic equation, and so judged will pass in the ritual of the ascension into a permanent light body. When a soul is found wanting, weighed in the exact mathematical equation of the use of energy, a deliberation ensues and there is a trial with an advocacy system. At the end of the proceeding, if the soul is still found wanting, the identity is immediately cancelled out in the Lake of Fire (energy), and the latent energy remaining is returned to the universal source for purification and redistribution.

Enlightenment. An eastern word for basically the same process as the ascension. This victory of the eightfold path was demonstrated by Gautama Buddha eight hundred years before Jesus' demonstration to the western consciousness.

Golden-Age Civilization. Soul lifewaves that achieved great heights working out their advancement and initiations over time as a group at various geographical points. Atlantis was such an advanced civilization and was located in a greater part of the Atlantic ocean basin, approximately 12,000 years ago, estimated by Churchward. Lemuria, located as a great continent in the Pacific, existed for about 250,000 years about 1,000,000 years ago, roughly estimated. These and other civilizations achieved great scientific advancement and direct contact with the hierarchies of light. These advanced civilizations succeeded for many thousands of years, but eventually collapsed when the battle of Armageddon accelerated through the infiltration of the Dark Force. However, many souls did achieve their personal victory and ascension and are part of the body of God working out further attainment and service in this and other sectors of the universe.

America — known as the home of the "I-AM-RACE" — is destined to be developed for another golden-age civilization.

Golden refers to the Christic light of the sun, and the unlimited source of energy in light in their cities of light.

Hard Music. Music designed for the destruction of the aura, the etheric blueprint, to interfere with the evolution of soul, to tear the aura and open this protective forcefield to drain energy. Rock music with its jagged rhythms and computerized, synthesized, mechanical beat is such an example, particularly acid rock. This music is seen with advanced vision as siphoning off, in a dark spiral vortex, energy from souls of light, as compared to divinely inspired music designed to uplift the soul.

Heart Center. The central energy center of the human soul, known also as the heart chakra. Chakra is an ancient Hindu word for these energy centers of which the human aura has seven lined up vertically along the spine. The heart is in the center with three above and three below and represents the cross-over point, the figure "8" energy flow. It is the point of transmutation — change of energy from a lower frequency to a higher, and is the point of purification. It is the point of connection with hierarchy and can be thought of as the cross, the crossing over to a higher plane of consciousness. It exists in the etheric envelope surrounding the physical body, located a few inches outside the location of the physical heart. It is the location of the threefold flame of the soul which burns inside this energy center in all souls of light. Correctly learning the science of intensifying this God-given flame is the key to soul evolution and mastery.

Hierarchy. The shorthand name given to the organizational aspect of advanced souls of light with higher initiations and attainment existing in light bodies in the etheric and higher planes of God's consciousness in his unlimited universe. Another shorthand is to call these souls saints, ascended beings, masters of time and space, angels, etc., and more formerly, the Great White Brotherhood. These beings no longer reside in physical bodies. There are, however, in this hierarchial chain, unascended souls of light of various levels of evolution that, by their conscious devotion and will, are recognized by their advanced brothers in the etheric.

Incarnation. Refers to one physical lifetime in which the soul descends into physical form of flesh and blood.

Initiations. Steps, waypoints in the mastery of the path of evolution, ritualized in the inner planes and on the outer, sometimes experienced as changes in one's life directions for a positive or negative choice.

Karmic Ties. Unfinished business with other souls from usually other lifetimes with whom misused energy needs balancing and forgiveness — *e.g.,* a murderer may need to experience being killed in another lifetime at the hand of his former victim, or at least have a contact with his former victim in which he may experience fear and helplessness; a stormy, failed marriage may need the opportunity for those two souls to meet again, resolve their karma and depart in peace.

Karmic Weight. A density measurable in part as an equivalent physical weight, also perceived as density in the aura registering upon the soul as darkness and upon the outer character form as changes in the physical form, *i.e.,* sickness, disease and perhaps death.

Planes of Consciousness.

 Physical Plane. Corresponds to the human form of mater, organic and inorganic substances; what one can see, feel and touch.

 Astral Plane. A plane of consciousness of a different frequency from the physical, but tied to the physical plane, and not visible by ordinary perceptions, but interpenetrates the physical plane. It contains all of man's miscreations of consciousness where they are stored and contained from contaminating the greater universe. It is the repository of all negative thoughtforms, emotions, *i.e.,* anger, rage, hate, lust, etc., and their reciprocal creations in fantasy form that are maintained in the astral plane.

Souls lacking sufficient spiritual consciousness and not tethered to higher etheric planes are automatically, by their density, entrapped in the astral plane on passing through the phenomenon known to man as death. Each religion has a different name for this plane — hell, purgatory of the Catholic, Judao-Christian belief; the bardo of the Tibetan Buddhist. These souls may await reembodiment from this plane if they are not rescued by angels under direct order from more aware souls in embodiment. On rescue they will be taken to the etheric retreats and schools for further training and preparation for another reembodiment, a reembodiment that will be tailored to assist in their soul evolution and opportunity for mastery.

Etheric Plane. Planes of higher states of God's consciousness, an advanced frequency penetrable only by attainment of the soul. It is the location of etheric schools of light, etheric retreats for further training and service. It is also the location of the permanent part of the soul, the angel of each one's Presence and the auric light of attainment seen as concentric rings of fire surrounding the God Presence of the soul.

Psychoanalyst. A medical doctor trained in the medical specialty of psychiatry and additionally trained in the sub-specialty of psychoanalysis with special knowledge of the man's lower mind originally codified in the work of Freud, Jung and Reich, *et al,* and applies an understanding of the unconscious and dream symbols to assist in the integration of the unconscious and conscious mind of the psyche.

Reembodied Atlantean Scientists. Scientists — certain souls returning at this time to rework their karma by appearing once again as modern scientists to be given their final opportunity of undoing their miscreations of energy while embodied in Atlantis. Their miscreations of that time were, by the use of an advanced knowledge of DNA, the manufacturing of servants in the form of humanoids, robots, insects, animals and animal-human combinations, some of which are leftover to this day. This was a clear disobedience to the cosmic law and these aberrant forms were used as weapons against man and representatives of God. So far many of these souls returning have not yet learned their karmic lesson, which was the destruction of Atlantis, and are today rapidly recreating their original destructive misuse of science here in America. Cataclysm, earthquakte, elemental disturbance resulted in the sinking of Atlantis, recorded in the Bible as a flood (Gen. 7). Lemuria was destroyed by nuclear fire and earthquake.

Reincarnation. A soul reembodies again and again for evolution and soul mastery over time and space.

Saline Abortion. A medically accepted technique for aborting pregnancy of over three months' term when it is no longer possible to terminate by a dilatation and curettage, a D & C surgery. This technique uses the introduction of a long, sterile needle directly into the amniotic sac — the protective fluid envelope surrounding the child inside the uterus. A saline salt solution is introduced through this needle and acts as a caustic agent similar to acid on the surface of the fetus, and causes great pain to the child. To escape this irritant the struggling child secondarily excites the uterus. An abrupt, intensive labor ensues and the child is delivered, alive or dead, frequently alive, only to gaspingly die from lungs prematurely developed or from the shock of scaled-burned skin. Some, however, refuse to die.

Sanat Kumara. Hierarch of Venus, known in Bible as the Ancient of Days — revealed unto Daniel (Dan. 7:9, 13, 22).

An ageless, advanced soul of great light who represents the Godhead for this sector of the universe. With the fall of the fourth root race, there was not a single soul left upon the planet with sufficient light left in the aura — a flame in the heart center to sustain evolution. By law the Cosmic Council, therefore, decreed the dissolution of the planet. Sanat Kumara, hearing this, went before the Council and pledged his light attainment as collateral and stated he would descend to earth until someone among the soul evolutions would come forward to take his place. This dispensation was granted but, by cosmic law, could only be granted one time, and this only for a certain cycle of time. And ready or not, mankind's group karma would then have to return.

Soul Lifewaves. Large number of souls bound together to work out karma individually as a group. These lifewaves and their evolution are overseen by advanced hierarchial beings, and their cycles of embodiment are governed by cosmic law. The planet earth has had so far six root races in embodiment. The first, second, and third races all achieved their ascension and mastery and no longer need the planet earth as a base for their evolution. They are now part of the governing hierarchy of light in the etheric planes. The fourth root race, however, did not ascend as a group. Biblical history records their fall from a protected geographical location known as Eden (Gen. 3:23), a mystery school in the physical plane but anchored in the etheric of the planet earth. This fall was into a dense consciousness and a dark struggle with the density of the physical plane. A few of this group, however, have ascended, but the balance are still using the planet as a base for their evolution. The result of this fall from consciousness and perfection opened the protection of light around the soul group evolving on the planet. This opened the planet's forcefield to other evolutions, and another older soul lifewave was allowed to share the planet as a base for their continued evolution. This lifewave is the remaining one-third left over from a self-destroyed planet, Maldek, a lifewave known as laggard souls for their slowness and recalcitrance to evolve and to learn obedience to cosmic law.

Along with the laggard soul evolution, also came the fallen angels, evolutions who have been committed to a complete conscious path of rebellion and have little light left in their soul sheath. They are known as fallen ones — fallen because eons ago they had achieved great mastery and attainment before their rebellion and fall into density (Isa. 14:12). This story has been repeated many times on other planets and systems of worlds.

The fifth root race of souls then also embodied along with the majority of the remaining fourth, and they too failed as a group, partly because of the extensive infiltration by the fallen ones and their seeming superior knowledge in the ways of the physical plane, and the ways of the world. And this is the basis for the statement and parable of the master Jesus about the difficulty of separation of the tares and the wheat, until the field is white for the harvest [the judgment] (John 4:35).

The sixth root race, now almost completely in embodiment, appears to be following the failed path of the fourth and fifth in a group failure.

The seventh root race, the last scheduled to use the planet earth, is still waiting in the etheric cities and retreats for their opportunity for embodiment. They are an advanced race, and are to embody for the most part in South America.

Transmutation. The changing of energy from one form to another — often from matter to spirit, or from spirit to matter — as practiced by the ancient alchemists. Today a special dispensation has returned to the planet, not known since the fall of Lemuria — the technique for transforming karmic weight, density, registering as darkness upon the aura into light that is retained and stored in the higher light body of the soul. This light can then be drawn on for further good works at will. This technique uses the invocative science of calling on the Lord and visualization of the violet seventh ray energy to convert darkness and karma into useful light.

Discernment
Discrimination
Determination
Descipline

Sacrifice
Selflessness
Service
Surrender